People Who Changed the Course of History

The Story of

Queen Victoria

200 YEARS AFTER HER BIRTH

By Danielle Thorne

PEOPLE WHO CHANGED THE COURSE OF HISTORY: THE STORY OF QUEEN VICTORIA 200 YEARS AFTER HER BIRTH

1405 SW 6th Avenue • Ocala, Florida 34471 • Phone 800-814-1132 • Fax 352-622-1875
Website: www.atlantic-pub.com • Email: sales@atlantic-pub.com
SAN Number: 268-1250

Library of Congress Cataloging-in-Publication Data

Names: Thorne, Danielle, author
Title: The story of Queen Victoria 200 years after her birth : people who changed the course of history / by Danielle Thorne.
Other titles: Story of Queen Victoria two hundred years after her birth
Description: Ocala, Florida : Atlantic Publishing Group, 2017. | Series: People Who changed the course of history | Includes bibliographical references and index.
Identifiers: LCCN 2018006510 (print) | LCCN 2018020044 (ebook) | ISBN 9781620235317 (ebook) | ISBN 9781620235300 (pbk. : alk. paper) | ISBN 9781620235324 (library edition : alk. paper) | ISBN 1620235307 (alk. paper)
Subjects: LCSH: Victoria, Queen of Great Britain, 1819-1901. | Queens--Great Britain--Biography. | Great Britain--History--Victoria, 1837-1901.
Classification: LCC DA554 (ebook) | LCC DA554 .T56 2018 (print) | DDC 941.081092 [B] --dc23
LC record available at https://lccn.loc.gov/2018006510

Printed in the United States

PROJECT MANAGER: Danielle Lieneman
INTERIOR LAYOUT AND JACKET DESIGN: Nicole Sturk

Reduce. Reuse.
RECYCLE.

Over the years, we have adopted a number of dogs from rescues and shelters. First there was Bear and after he passed, Ginger and Scout. Now, we have Kira, another rescue. They have brought immense joy and love not just into our lives, but into the lives of all who met them.

We want you to know a portion of the profits of this book will be donated in Bear, Ginger and Scout's memory to local animal shelters, parks, conservation organizations, and other individuals and nonprofit organizations in need of assistance.

– Douglas & Sherri Brown,
President & Vice-President of Atlantic Publishing

Table of Contents

Once There Was a Princess

A little girl curls her legs beneath herself while she plays with toys on the floor. Surrounded by dozens of dolls dressed in fine, handmade clothes, she almost looks like one of them with her light hair, round blue eyes, and chubby cheeks.

"Oh dear," she croons to the one in her arms, "you have been naughty three different times today. Now promise Mama you will be very good and need no scolding tomorrow if she's kind to you."

Nearby, on a soft-covered footstool, her governess laughs. She calls her "Little Drina" in German, then reminds the little girl that one must be very good whether Mama and the others are kind or not. The spoiled child responds, "Mama is cross with me. Yesterday I told Jane she may not touch my dolls because they are all mine, and she complained."

"Perhaps you should share your things, Victoria. Most little girls don't have as many playthings as do you."

"Why should I share them," the perplexed princess frowns, "for I can call Lady Ellice by her name, but she may not call me by mine."

The governess remains silent at this remark, for the little girl playing in the enormous bedchamber is right after all. She may not be addressed as "Victoria" by visitors, and she does not have to share her things if she does not wish to do so. After all, should things work out as many of England's politicians and peers suspect, the charming, but headstrong child playing with her dolls on the thick carpet might someday become Queen of England.

A portrait of Victoria at four years old by Stephen Poyntz Denning, 1823.

Queen Victoria of England is one of the greatest success stories in the history of the English throne. She became a teen queen when she was 18 years old and ruled the United Kingdom peacefully for 63 years. Her reign was longer than any **monarch** that came before her or any that followed, until the current Queen of England, Queen Elizabeth II, broke the record in 2015.

Christened **Princess Alexandrina Victoria**, Queen Victoria came into the world at Kensington Palace in London on May 14, 1819. Her mother was a German princess, her father the **Duke of Kent**. Her grandfather, **George III**, was King of England the day she was born.

As a little princess, Queen Victoria was a distant fifth in line to the throne. Those who disliked her German mother or were also close to inheriting the crown saw her as a threat. It would take years of planning, precautions, and a great deal of education to prepare a strong, confident woman who would win over England's governing body, **Parliament**, and earn the love of the people.

CHAPTER ONE

Queen Victoria's England

When Queen Victoria was born, becoming king or queen of England could be a complicated path. 66 kings and queens had ruled the country with different European backgrounds for the past 1,500 years![1]

FAST FACT

England has been known by a few different names throughout history. When Scotland joined England in 1707, the countries, including the area of Wales, were called Great Britain. Northern Ireland became a part of England and Scotland in 1801, and the name changed to the United Kingdom.

The "United Kingdom of Great Britain and Northern Ireland" is the official title for these countries today, but when going to London, most people still say they are going to visit England.

The earliest known conquerors of England were the Romans. Roman artifacts are still being discovered beneath England's soil today. After battling to stay in control of the natives, they soon abandoned the island.

---

1. Wilkinson, Philip. 2006

The next invaders were the **Anglo-Saxons**. They arrived after the Romans left. This mixed group of raiders came from Germany and the Danish **peninsula**. After fighting the inhabitants for control and squabbling among themselves for kingdoms and power, the Anglos had to contend with new invaders: **Vikings**.

The Vikings sailed to English shores from Scandinavia, which is today's Denmark, Finland, and Norway. They were vicious raiders who loved to fight and steal. Some settled down and turned to trading, but the goal of the Vikings was to rule England.

In the late 800s A.D., an army of 10,000 Vikings set sail to conquer England once and for all, but a terrible storm ruined their plans. They didn't make it. Eventually, there was peace, but the fight over ruling England wasn't over.

War seemed to be a part of life for the early people of England. The arrival of the **Normans** was the last major group of warriors who came to England with the intent of capturing it for themselves. This group of conquerors came from northern France. After many battles and a great amount of bloodshed, they gained control of the country and crowned **William the Conqueror** as king in 1066.

FAST FACT

The House of Tudor resolved much of the fighting for control within England when it took control in 1485 under Henry VII. Four more Tudors followed: Henry VIII, Edward VI, Mary I, and Elizabeth I. Afterward, the throne was passed to the House of Stuart. Victoria's house, the House of Hanover, would gain power in 1714 under George I.

The Normans ruled for about a century — that's 100 years. Eventually, after much fighting for power, the people of England settled into a pattern of passing the crown down from one family generation to the next.

William the Conqueror poses for an Anglo-Saxon style art portrait painted with oil on panel.

THE HOUSE OF HANOVER

Victoria was descended from the **House of Hanover**, a German branch of royalty that ruled England beginning in 1714, about 100 years before Victoria was born. Hanover began as a fishing village, then a town, and later became a ruling city of the area we know today as Germany.

George I was the first king of the House of Hanover to rule England. He inherited the throne after Queen Anne died with no children that could inherit the crown. George I was related to Queen Anne's family that ruled during the time of the **Stuart** family, but he was born in Hanover and didn't speak English.

The people of England weren't crazy about having a German king who was already 54 years old. This Protestant king did not spend a lot of time in England, which made it easier for the Catholics to rebel. King George I had to squash a rebellion in Scotland and later deal with the South Sea Bubble crisis that ruined the economy and many families in 1720.

(Left) King George I poses for a detail portrait painted by Godfrey Kneller.
(Right) King George II poses for an oil on canvas painting by Charles Jervas.

FAST FACT

The South Sea Bubble is remembered as being the first stock market crash, and it happened during the reign of the first king, George I, from the House of Hanover. It began when Parliament passed a bill to allow only the South Sea Company to trade in South America. In return, the government was loaned £7 million. Stock, or parts of the company for sale, rose in value and everyone hurried to invest their money. But the South Sea Company did not work out. Worse, some investments into it were legitimate, but some were scams. Thousands of people were affected and some lost everything.

George II was the second ruler of the House of Hanover. He became king in his forties when his father died unexpectedly in 1727. George II had been born in Hanover, too, but he spoke English. In fact, he grew up translating for his father in royal court and meetings. George II had experience as a military leader and government employee. During his reign, he dealt with wars in Spain, Austria, and other countries in Europe. His experiences made him a respected and successful leader. When he died, he passed the throne on to his grandson, George III, because his first-born son, Fred, had already died.

George III was the grandfather of Queen Victoria. He ruled from 1760 to 1820. His reign was influenced by Napoleon Bonaparte and the long wars with the French emperor who wanted to rule the world. He also ruled during the American Revolution and was blamed for losing the war.

At home, King George III loved to study the advances of agriculture. He wrote articles under a fake name about farming, and he ordered improvements on the royal fields. The House of Hanover often chose German husbands and wives from noble families to bring to England. After marrying Charlotte of Mecklenburg, who also had German roots, George III had 15 children.

This photo of King George III hangs in the National Portrait Gallery in London, and features the king wearing a red coat, which is similar to the ones his soldiers wore during the Revolutionary War.

Queen Victoria was the last English monarch to rule from the House of Hanover. After she died in 1901, her son, Edward took the throne and the ruling name of the dynasty changed to the House of Saxe-Coburg-Gotha. This was because Edward had taken his father's name, but some people thought it sounded too German. The name was changed to the House of Windsor, which is the ruling house today.

(Left) The coat of arms of the House of Saxe-Coburg-Gotha during Edward VII's reign (1901-1910). (Right) The Badge of the House of Windsor was approved by King George VI in 1938, and this particular style has been used since 1952.

The House of Hanover ruled during an important time in England's history. The kingdom grew as it conquered or governed more and more countries around the world. There was a boom in agricultural studies and improvements as science evolved. The Industrial Revolution brought a surge in employment and to the economy. More attention and solutions were sought out for those struggling with poverty and disease. Not all of these wonders are attributed to Victoria's reign, which had its share of ups and downs, but the family dynasty brought about great and positive changes.

Primogeniture

On Queen Victoria's birthday, she was fifth in line to the throne. In other words, there were five other people, mostly uncles, between the crown and herself. Her grandfather, King George III, was the ruler at the time of her birth. He and his wife, **Queen Charlotte**, had 12 living children plus three who had died. Of the children still living, seven were boys and five were girls.

FAST FACT

Even though King George had 12 heirs at the time Victoria was born, the crown would go to his sons and even to *their* children first, before it would pass to any of the king's daughters. This is called primogeniture.

The other living royals between King George III and Victoria were George IV, the first-born son of the king; the king's next two sons, Frederick and William; and then Victoria's father, Edward. He was son number four. Next to claim the crown after Edward was the newborn Victoria.

George IV, Prince Regent

George IV began to rule as **Prince Regent** before his father died because King George III suffered from a mental illness. A regent rules in place of a king or queen that is still living. The new Prince Regent took over the throne and made the best of it. This new king liked to have nice things. His bills for clothes, jewels, parties, and homes became so high that he couldn't pay them. His elaborate style became popular in art, design, and architecture and came to be known as the **Regency** style.

In this portrait by Henry Bone, Prince Regent George IV wears the red uniform of a Field-Marshal, wearing several badges to signify different ranks and honors.

George IV did not want to marry just to find a queen. He wed a woman he loved, although she was a **commoner**, a widow, and a Catholic, all unacceptable for someone on the throne. The marriage wasn't considered to be the real thing, so he was forced to marry **Caroline of Brunswick**. Neither was ever happy with the other.

This engraved portrait of Caroline of Brunswick by James Tookey in 1795 hangs in the National Portrait Gallery today.

FAST FACT

Catholics and Protestants persecuted one another for much of England's history. It usually depended upon whether the ruling monarch was Catholic or Protestant and what changes were made to the laws. Queen Victoria was a Protestant.

Princess Charlotte

The Prince Regent did have one child with his official wife. The baby's name was Charlotte, just like the Prince Regent's mother. Princess Charlotte was popular with the people because of her good looks and personality. She married a German, **Prince Leopold of Saxe-Coburg-Saalfeld**.

Prince Leopold was Victoria's uncle from her mother's family. Leopold would one day become King of Belgium, and he and Victoria would remain very close throughout their lives.

Unfortunately Princess Charlotte died after giving birth to her own first child in November of 1817. The baby died, too. It was two years before Victoria came along. With no living children, this meant that when the Prince Regent, George IV, died, the crown would go next to his brother, Frederick, if he survived.

Princess Charlotte is featured here with her husband
King Leopold I.

Frederick, Duke of York

Frederick was the second son of King George III, and he was in line for the throne after the Prince Regent. Titled the **Duke of York**, he married a princess of Prussia in 1791 when he was 28 years old. Frederick joined the army when he was 17 and served for many years, making positive changes and reorganizations to the military. He also fought in the French Revolution. Frederick did not have any children before he died in 1827. Victoria was seven years old.

This portrait features Prince Frederick, Duke of York and Albany, who was the namesake of the state of New York and its capital, Albany.

FAST FACT

In the middle of the 19th century, most people only lived to be about 40 years old.[2]

William IV

After Frederick, William was the next brother in line to inherit the throne. Frederick died before he could have a chance to sit on the throne, so William became king after the death of his brother, George IV. William IV was quite elderly for a king. He became the monarch at 64 years old. Because he was a younger son, he did not grow up thinking about the crown. Instead, he joined the Navy as an ordinary seaman. Throughout the years, he rose up to become **Admiral of the Fleet**.

William IV didn't marry while in his youth. Instead, he had 10 children with a stage actress, but they were not considered royal heirs. With the death of so many royals in line for the throne, William soon realized he must find a royal wife. He married the daughter of a German duke when he was 52 years old. Unfortunately, none of their children lived, and William left behind no heirs when he died in 1837 after a 10-year rule. In a perfect coincidence, Victoria was 18 years old at the time of his death and officially old enough to rule on her own.

2. Baird, Julia. 2017.

This portrait of William IV was painted with oil on panel by artist Martin Archer Shee.

Edward, Duke of Kent

Had Victoria's father, the Duke of Kent, not died when she was a baby, he would have inherited the throne after his older brother, William the IV. Edward was thrilled with his adorable and healthy baby. Anxious to be near the seaside because of its healthy effects, he decided to take his wife and little girl to stay in a cottage at Devonshire in southwest England.

FAST FACT

Bloodletting was practiced by doctors for thousands of years, even during Victoria's lifetime. This medical procedure involved making a cut into a vein and bleeding into a cup or bowl to rid the body of bad or poisonous things. It's believed bloodletting began in Egypt then spread to Greece. Sometimes leeches would be used instead of sharp instruments. Doctors in the early 19th century used bloodletting and leeches to treat their patients all the time, although many patients became so weak from loss of blood that they died.

It was a very cold winter, and although Victoria managed very well in the harsh weather, the duke caught a fever after walking outdoors in the wind. He became violently ill and was bled repeatedly by doctors, which probably made him worse. The duke died on January 23, 1820, before his daughter had her very first birthday.

Edward, Duke of Kent and Strathearn, depicted here in 1818,
just two years before his death.

ENGLAND 1820

At the time of Queen Victoria's birth, many English wars around the world had ended. The **War of 1812** that fought over land and trade with the United States was over. Before long, the American President, James Monroe, would write the **Monroe Doctrine** and demand an end to England and Europe interfering with the western part of the world.

The long war between England and France was finally finished, too. The **Napoleonic Wars** began in 1799 when France's emperor, **Napoleon Bonaparte**, tried to take over Europe. England became involved in 1803 to protect its allies and eventually itself. The allies were successful. The Napoleonic Wars ended in 1815 when Bonaparte was defeated and sent into **exile**. England's war with France lasted over a decade, and it cost the lives of millions of English soldiers and sailors.

FAST FACT

The famous emperor of France, Napoleon Bonaparte, would never meet Queen Victoria. He died in 1821 when she was about two years old. Nearly 30 years later, Victoria would have a strong relationship with France and considered herself a good friend of Empress Eugenie and Prince Louis Napoleon Bonaparte, the nephew of Napoleon Bonaparte and the new ruler of the country.

By the time Victoria was born in 1819, the future looked brighter in some ways than it had at the beginning of the 19th century, but there was still a great deal of poverty. One exciting change was the new ideas about how to **manufacture goods** arriving from England's overseas world trade. A new kind of revolution was unfolding. It was change, not war, and it began to progress steadily in England during the queen's childhood.

FAST FACT

England built the greatest naval power in the world. In 1802, at the start of England's involvement with the Napoleonic Wars, it had an estimated 19,772 vessels. By 1815, there were almost 22,000 ships.[3] This enormous effort to build and sail wooden ships gave England over three times the advantage in battle over other countries like France and Spain, who had smaller navies.

Modern inventors and businessmen wanted a way to produce goods faster than the time it took to make things by hand. New, bigger machines were invented. The field of science, especially chemistry, advanced in a way that would help the new tools and machinery. The healthy economy of England seemed to explode with work and readily available products like ready-to-wear clothing and pottery.

FAST FACT

The Industrial Revolution took place between 1760 and 1840. Iron, steel, coal, steam, and petroleum changed the way things were made and inspired new inventions. It spread to America, too.

The era was dubbed the **Industrial Revolution**. Even though it did not completely solve poverty and created different problems, it was an age the future queen, and the world, would come to embrace.

---

3. Britannica.com. 2017.

THE ROYAL FAMILY

It may be surprising to learn that Queen Victoria's grandparents, King George III and his wife, Queen Charlotte, were considered quiet, no nonsense rulers for most of their lives. Victoria's grandparents led England through the Revolutionary War in America, the Napoleonic Wars, and the new industrial changes in England.

During this time, King George III became mentally ill, beginning with his loss of the American colonies. By 1811 he was no longer fit to rule because he'd lost his sight, health, and sanity. His first son took his place, but it was his fourth son, Edward, Duke of Kent, who would provide the next heir.

DID YOU KNOW?

In 1819, the year Victoria was born, many interesting inventions and discoveries were made:

- The doctor's stethoscope was invented by René Laënnec
- The wildly popular soda fountain was patented by Samuel Fahnestock
- Desolation Island in the Antarctic was discovered by Captain William Smith
- The first account of hay fever (allergies) was published by English physician John Bostock

LITTLE DRINA

Queen Victoria was born on a damp but quiet spring day in London. Healthy and stout, she was the third child of her mother, **Princess Victoire of Saxe-Coburg-Saalfeld**. It was very lucky that Victoria was born in England at all because her parents had just moved from Germany.

Little Drina's mother, Princess Victoire, was later named the Duchess of Nemours.

Victoria's father was not a young man. Although he was the son of King George III, he did not think he needed an heir because he had older brothers. This changed when he and his brother grew older and there weren't any royal grandchildren. There was also an interesting change in the rules. **The Settlement Act of 1701** changed laws so that a daughter could be queen if she didn't have any brothers. The Duke of Kent went to Germany to find a wife.

The duke knew that it was important for his child be born in the country where he or she might grow up to inherit the throne. He arrived in London with his German bride less than a month before Victoria's arrival. It was just in time.

Only a few weeks later, at Kensington Palace, many important people were called to the red brick palace because it looked like Victoria would be born. They were members of the **Privy Council,** a group of important men who met and discussed matters of England with the ruling king or queen. It was tradition for the Council to see and inspect a new royal baby, and after they left, the little family was finally left alone with their new daughter.

Although the everyday people of England did not pay much attention to Victoria's birth at the time, the announcement spread quickly among other royals and aristocrats that a new princess had arrived. Usually a new prince or princess was happy news, but sometimes it caused jealousy and crafty schemes.

Victoria was born at a time when children did not live very long. Quality healthcare was lacking, especially for the poor, and many people lived in dirty environments that caused or carried disease. Some busy mothers would drug their crying babies with opium to calm them, and though it was socially acceptable, this led to addiction and death.

FAST FACT

In the 1800s, new babies had a 30 percent chance of dying before their fifth birthday.[4] This means that three out of every 10 children died before they turned five years old.

The future queen's parents named her Alexandrina. Her second name would be Victoria, although her mother wanted it to be Charlotte. Alexandrina was a mouthful, so when the princess was little, everyone around her called her "Drina." She wouldn't be called "Victoria" until she was five years old.

FAST FACT

Queen Victoria was only four feet and eleven inches tall by the time she was sixteen years old.[5]

Drina was not a sickly baby. Her enormous blue eyes and short, solid body gave her the appearance of a strong little soldier. She took after her father's looks with her round face and eyes, and she would never be tall.

Everyone was charmed by little Drina's looks and personality, and she quickly became the favorite at Kensington Palace. This meant she was spoiled, and it showed in her demeanor. Even when she was very young, it was said she had a bad temper and an attitude that hinted she knew she would be queen.

---

4. Baird, Julia. 2017.
5. Baird, Julia. 2017

A portrait of a young Victoria with her mother, the Duchess of Kent.

In fact, historical journals report that Victoria acted pretty tough for a baby when she cut her first teeth. She soon showed signs of stubbornness when she didn't get her way. It was the early beginnings of a reputation for the strong determination that she would be known for the rest of her life.

FAST FACT

Sir Walter Scott, the famous writer, wrote that even though she was kept from knowing who she was while she was a child, he suspected that "…if we could dissect the little heart, we should find some pigeon or other bird of the air had carried the matter,"[6] to the young Victoria.

Unfortunately, after Victoria's peaceful arrival into the world things took a turn for the worse. The first tragedy in Victoria's life was the death of her father before her first birthday. She was only eight months old when he became sick after a walk out in cold, windy weather. He died on January 23, 1820. This left the Duchess of Kent alone in a country foreign to her, where many people did not like or trust her because she was German.

More terrible news arrived. Less than a week after the death of the Duke of Kent, the ruling monarch, King George III, also died. In less than a month the new princess had lost her father and grandfather.

Sadly, not everyone thought this was bad news. There were people around Victoria that became more concerned with what this meant for the princess's future rather than considering how it would feel to grow up without a father and grandfather. People realized Victoria could be queen someday and that meant power and money for those closest to her.

Poor little Drina. She'd moved from fifth to third in line to the throne of England, and she was just a newborn baby.

---

6. Baird, Julia 2017.

CHAPTER 2

Fierce but Lonely

Queen Victoria, or little Drina, quickly became a favorite of the Kensington Palace household, although many of her aunts and uncles in line for the throne did not like her. Because of rumors that her life might be in danger, she was watched closely and never left alone. It was all for her safety of course, but she became very spoiled. It should come as no surprise that Victoria did not have a normal childhood. Sadly, she did not even have a normal relationship with her parents.

There were many rules in her life she had to obey as a child, and Victoria let everyone know that she hated them. She could not play with other children. She was never alone, even when she slept in her room at night. Victoria had to learn to sit still for long periods of time, take medicine, practice her piano, and do her studies. Everything in Victoria's life was a rule or an order.

FAST FACT

Victoria would stand at attention and scream as long and as loud as she could every time she saw her uncle, the Duke of Sussex. The duke lived upstairs in Kensington Palace, and someone close to Victoria threatened her that the he would punish her if he caught her being naughty. Rather than behave, Victoria shrieked like a storm whenever he came into view. Some people thought she was afraid. Some people thought it was a dare.

Unfortunately for Victoria, regular temper tantrums didn't change the rules, but it did mean Victoria was called "naughty" so many times that she wrote stories about naughty little girls. By the time she was 10 years old, Victoria was forced to write about her bad temper in a conduct book every day. She did so with enthusiasm, sometimes underlining words like "very" and "naughty."

Although childhood was tough, there was a great deal of privilege that came along with being a princess. Growing up, Victoria loved to play with her enormous collection of dolls, spend time with her grandmother, visit the palace horses, and play with her many pets. She wore beautiful clothes and took trips to the seaside with her mother and governess. The little princess had everything a child could wish for — except for friends or brothers and sisters close to her age. Once she was grown, Victoria often told her own children stories about how hard it was to grow up without any other close family around.

FATHER AND MOTHER

Victoria did not record much about her father, Edward, in her journal and letters since she did not grow up with him, but everyone knew the aging duke loved his daughter. He liked to brag that Victoria was as beautiful as she was strong and called her his "pocket Hercules."

FAST FACT

The mythical Greek god, Hercules, was a son of Zeus. Half-mortal, he was known for his amazing strength and courage.

At six feet tall, Victoria's father stood higher than average. (In the 1870s, the average height of an Englishman was just five foot five inches.[7]) He was proud of his health and his stature. He liked to believe that he was the strongest of the king's children and told everyone so.

Although he boasted about his health and appearance, the Duke of Kent did not behave wildly and selfishly like some of his older brothers. Following his parents' example, he disciplined himself and focused on a military career. He was the first royal to live in North America, where he lived in Canada and served as Commander-and-Chief of British forces. He educated himself so that he could form political opinions he believed would help his people.

The duke did not believe in slavery and defended the early ideas that every man should be free. He also defended the rights of Catholics in England who were persecuted at the time. Books were important to him. He had a collection of over 5,000 and even traveled with them.

Because he was fourth in line to the throne, the Duke of Kent did not think it was important to marry young and have heirs. He waited until was 51 years old. He loved his wife and felt like they had a good relationship. Before he passed away of his unexpected winter illness, he held her hand and asked her not to forget him. He left everything to the duchess in his will, but as a fourth son, his royal allowance was small, and he'd spent more than he had. This left the duchess with debt and very little to live on.

---

7. Gallop, Adrian.

Prince Edward stands next to his brother, Prince William,
in a portrait by Benjamin West.

It was hard for everyone to accept that the healthiest of the heirs to the
throne had died. People found it strange and terrible that the duchess
should be widowed twice. Some people became suspicious that she might
have murdered him. She grieved deeply for the duke though. "I am hope-
lessly lost without my dearest Edward,"[8] she cried when he passed away.
She had her husband buried at Windsor on February 12, 1820, in an enormous coffin that measured seven feet long.

The German princess, **Victoire of Saxe-Coburg-Saalfeld**, was 32 years old
when she married the Duke of Kent. From southern Germany, Victoire
had brown curls and rosy cheeks. She first married **Charles, Prince of
Leiningen** when she was a teenager and had twp children: **Prince Carl** and
Princess Feodora. They would be Victoria's half-brother and sister.

8. Williams. Kate. 2008.

Victoire's first husband died in 1814 when little Feodora was seven years old and Carl was eight. She needed another protective, loving partner, and her brother, Prince Leopold, had married into England's royal family through Princess Charlotte. His connection to King George III meant that he could help find wives for the king's sons. Leopold arranged for Victoire to meet and accept the proposal from the Duke of Kent. They married in May 1818, a year before Victoria was born.

Victoire was now the Duchess of Kent. She and her new husband decided to move back to Germany after the royal marriage because it was cheaper to live there. The little family returned to England when the duchess was eight months pregnant with Victoria, so she would be born on the soil she might someday rule.

The duchess loved her new baby very much. She called her "little *Vichelchen*" and cared for her mostly by herself. After the duke died there was little money and nowhere for her to go. Her brother, Leopold, helped her with money, and the Prince Regent allowed her and the young Princess Victoria to remain at Kensington Palace. People distrusted the Duchess of Kent, who pretended to speak very little English. She had a heavy accent and had to practice her second language, but even then she was treated as an outcast.

Things between Victoria and her mother changed as the baby grew older. The duchess knew she needed to raise a proper, prepared princess who could be a successful queen. Victoria did not like her mother's strict rules. She hated being followed everywhere and never having any time alone. The future queen fought with her mother much of her life, but they finally made peace when Victoria had her own children.

The Duchess of Kent, painted by Richard Rothwell in 1832.

A BROTHER AND SISTER

Victoria knew her half-brother and half-sister from her mother's first marriage well, but they were much older than her and didn't always live nearby. Carl, also called Charles, was the third Prince of Leiningen. He was born 15 years before Victoria in 1804. They would never be close friends. Carl married in 1829 and returned to Germany to have a career in the army. He eventually became a lieutenant general, and later served as the first prime minister in a new German government.

Carl did try to be a good big brother. He often tried to referee the arguments between Victoria and her mother. The problem was that he usually took his mother's side. Victoria felt betrayed by her only brother on these occasions, but years later she grieved for him when he died in 1856.

Feodora moved to Kensington Palace with the Duke and Duchess of Kent right before Victoria was born. Although they were 12 years apart in age, the two sisters enjoyed one another's company and loved each other very much. Both of them were unhappy with the strict life and routine at Kensington, but they spent some happy times together talking and taking little trips to parks or the seashore.

Feodora had dark hair and eyes and a pretty little mouth. She was thought to be beautiful and clever, and she was always kind to her little sister. In 1828, when Victoria was almost nine years old, Feodora, only 21 years of age, married Prince Earnest of Hohenlohe-Langenburg. He did not have a lot of money or power, but Feodora thought he was handsome, and she was happy to escape back to Germany. She felt miserable leaving her little sister behind.

Victoria's sister, Feodora of Hohenlohe-Langenburg, posing for a portrait in 1838.

Victoria realized then she was truly alone and had a hard time dealing with it. The sisters wrote to each other regularly, and Feodora later returned to visit with her children. Victoria would be so upset when her sister and nieces and nephews departed that she would cry for hours. The young girl would scribble page after page in her diary about how wonderful they were and how much she missed them.

Feodora had six children with her husband, who died in 1860. Victoria's husband died around that time, too, and the sisters visited and grieved together. As the years passed, and family and friends around her began to pass away, Victoria prayed for her sister's health, saying she hoped desperately that God would preserve the only sister she'd ever had.

Feodora lived another 12 years before she became sick and died in 1872. The queen was broken-hearted to lose her only sister because she considered her an equal. Feodora left a loving note for Victoria, telling her,

> *"I can never thank you enough for all you have done for me, for your great love and tender affection. These feelings cannot die, they must and will live in my soul — till we meet again, never more to be separated..."*

GOVERNESS LEHZEN

Besides being guarded closely by her German mother, Victoria also had a **governess**. A governess is like a nanny, teacher, and friend all in one. Governesses in the 19th century helped raise little girls into proper young ladies.

While Victoria disliked her mother for guarding her like a prisoner, she was close to her governess, the **Baroness Louise Lehzen**. Lehzen was from

9. Martin. Theodore.

Germany, too. She first came to work for the family as a governess for Victoria's half-sister, Feodora, when Victoria was a baby. The devoted, single woman had dark hair and a kind expression. She worshiped Victoria.

Some people blamed Lehzen for Victoria's lifelong stubbornness, but Lehzen wanted to prepare Victoria for her royal duties. The German governess disciplined the little princess and did not mind her screaming at all. One letter from Victoria's half-sister reminded her that she would get so angry when they were little she would throw scissors at Lehzen. What a patient teacher!

Victoria drew this picture of Baroness Louise Lehzen in 1835
before the future queen's ascension to the throne.

Although it wasn't popular for women to be educated, a royal was different. The governess made sure Victoria had extensive schooling just like a young man. The future queen learned to read and work numbers, as well as speak different languages, including German, French, Italian, and Latin. Victoria also studied dance and appreciated art and music.

FAST FACT

In the early 19th century, children in England received very little education unless they were wealthy or aristocratic and could afford expensive public schooling. There were some church schools for boys, or they could choose to become apprentices and learn a trade. Girls, even in the upper classes, were not thought to need any formal education past basic reading and arithmetic. Instead, they practiced homemaking skills to prepare for marriage.

One day, when Victoria was 10 years old, she saw a map of British royalty. By this time, the princess was third in line to the throne. No one had told Victoria how close she was to becoming a queen, so she began to cry. Her governess told the royal household that the princess dried her tears and then held up her finger and announced, "I will be good."[10]

Lehzen never left Victoria's side during the years she was a governess. She guided Victoria through her teen years and into the position of Queen of England. Victoria always listened to Lehzen and trusted her advice. This kept Victoria safe, because she was all Lehzen truly cared about. Unfortunately, it made Lehzen many enemies.

Lehzen stayed with Victoria until after the young queen married. The governess and queen's new husband did not agree on how to take care of Victoria, and they argued about it on many occasions. Soon, they were jealous

10. Baird, Julia. 2017.

of each other and one could not say anything kind about the other. This put Victoria in the middle, which created tears and confusion.

After Victoria's second child was born, Lehzen returned to Germany. It was so hard to do that she left without saying goodbye. As queen, Victoria visited her once, but it was 24 years later.

Lehzen died in 1870 after living to be 85 years old. Victoria wrote of her, "I can never forget that she was for many years everything to me."

CONROY THE CONMAN

Victoria grew to dislike and distrust her mother throughout the years, mostly because of a man named Captain John Conroy. Conroy was once a solider, and he worked for Victoria's father until he died. He became an advisor to the duchess and a part of the family. Conroy loved that the duchess trusted him and that Victoria might someday be queen. He took advantage of his role as an advisor and tried to control everything the duchess and Victoria did so he would be important to the future queen and her mother.

The duchess and Conroy developed a special relationship. Although no one else trusted him, the duchess seemed to fall under a spell and would do everything he suggested to keep Victoria under their control. The young princess was cut off from family and friends, even her uncle, King William IV, who loved her and enjoyed her company. Conroy also fired a lady-in-waiting to the duchess, whom Victoria loved, after accusing the lady of spying for the king. This prevented Victoria from growing close to anyone on the household staff and forced her to rely on Conroy.

Sir John Conroy poses here for an oil on canvas portrait.

FAST FACT

The day Victoria became queen, John Conroy demanded a title and £3,000 a year. That's equal to over $1 million today. Victoria quickly booted him out of the house and out of her life. To keep the peace, the prime minister promised him a bit of money and gave him the title of Baronet. Conroy spent the rest of his life trying to get his revenge.

Conroy won all of his arguments by telling everyone Victoria was in danger of being kidnapped or poisoned. What he really wanted was to be made Private Secretary to Victoria if she ever inherited the throne. Once, when Victoria became very ill, Conroy forced a pen in her hand and tried to make her sign a decree that would make him her secretary. Victoria fought him, even as her mother watched and did nothing. After many weeks, Victoria recovered, but she could hardly walk, and she lost a lot of her hair. Victoria never forgave Conroy, and it took years before she would trust her mother again.

UNCLE LEOPOLD

Another member of Victoria's family that influenced her life was Uncle Leopold. Prince Leopold of Saxe-Coburg-Saalfeld was the German brother of Victoria's mother. He understood English history and laws from his own marriage and tried to help his sister and niece survive in England.

Leopold kept a home called **Claremont** in Surry, England. Throughout his life, he tried to take the place of Victoria's father by writing her letters, visiting often, and giving her good advice. He introduced his nephew, Albert, to Victoria because he thought they'd make a good couple.

Uncle Leopold became king of Belgium in July 1831, when Victoria
was just 12 years old.

Leopold was handsome, kind, and cared about all of his family. He knew Victoria had a difficult childhood because she was a princess. He did not trust the people around Victoria who wanted to use her to gain their own power. Leopold helped his newborn niece with finances after her father died. He called Victoria his "dear little chicken" and encouraged her to study and get regular exercise. He took Victoria and her mother on trips or visited them. Victoria would sob when he returned home.

FAST FACT

Victoria was an avid letter writer. She also kept detailed diaries her entire life. In one of them, she wrote about how much Leopold helped her. She said, "He is indeed like my real father, as I have none!"[11]

Later, Leopold encouraged her match in a husband. He went on to listen and advise her on marriage and family and her specific responsibilities as a leader of the United Kingdom. Leopold's lessons helped Victoria be a good queen by teaching her to be humble but determined and giving her an understanding of the importance of history and responsibility. They exchanged letters regularly up until he passed away in 1865.

DASH THE DOG

There were *some* special things about her childhood that Victoria treasured. Her dog, Dash, was one friend she could count on, and Victoria loved to play with him. Dash was a small black and white King Charles Spaniel. Although he was given to Victoria's mother as a gift, the princess fell in love with him, and they became close friends.

---

11. Williams, Kate. 2008.

FAST FACT

The King Charles Spaniel is a small dog that is friendly and easy to train. They only grow up to 18 pounds but can live as long as 15 years. They're affectionate, and they like other dogs and small children. This breed is gentle and sweet. It's still quite popular in England today.

The princess spoiled Dash with Christmas presents, and he followed her around whenever he could. Her trusted companion lived 10 years before dying in 1840. He is buried in Windsor Home Park with a marker etched with a poem that is all about him.

THE POPULAR LITTLE ROYAL

As Victoria grew, her older uncles died one by one, and she became closer to wearing the crown. All of a sudden, the people of the United Kingdom began to pay more attention to the girl who might one day be queen.

By 1830, when her uncle, William IV, ruled, factories were cropping up in small cities which made them bigger and more crowded. New towns were formed. The countryside became stained with black dust, caused by mining and burning coal.

A middle class grew, but so did health problems, political problems, and extreme poverty for the lower classes. Another important change that affected the world occurred in 1833 when England abolished slavery. The English began to understand the importance of human rights.

All of the growth and changes made a big impact. Riots became more frequent. Because cities with factories were growing in population, people became angry they did not have the **representation** they deserved. Government leaders worried there might be a revolution like what had happened in France. Because of this, some amazing changes began to happen in the government.

Apart from having a royal ruler, England's people were also represented in Parliament. Similar to the United States' Congress, Parliament had two groups of representatives. **The House of Commons** were men who were voted to represent regular people, called **commoners**. The other house was called **The House of Lords**. This group had aristocratic, wealthy representatives who had titles or inherited their seats. Together, these houses worked with a leader chosen from the ruling party, called the **prime minister**, who reported to and worked with the king or queen.

For the first time in history, the House of Commons grew and passed the House of Lords in size and influence. The **Whig** party, a more tolerant group, came into power. England was ready for changes in society and in how their government functioned.

FAST FACT

There are two main political parties in English history: the Tories and the Whigs. The Tories formed in the late 1670s. A tory was conservative and supported having a monarch that had nearly absolute power. The Whig party formed around the 1680s. Whigs did not want to be ruled only by a monarch. They preferred a constitutional monarchy, which meant the people would have representatives who would run the country alongside a king or queen.

Victoria was going through changes of her own. Because her Uncle William became king at 64, it wouldn't be long before she was queen. Parliament realized she needed a good allowance to continue her education and run a proper household with tutors and servants.

The queen-to-be was given a 10,000 pound allowance to prepare herself. Of course, the money was controlled by the duchess and Captain Conroy, but Victoria began to travel more so that she could see how everyday people lived and so the people of England could get to know her better in return. Her keepers took her on a long tour with welcoming parties and balls where she became an instant celebrity.

The teenage princess was shocked by the appearance and living conditions of the poor. She felt uncomfortable seeing dirty, sick people, especially the rowdy and drunk. Although she loved having more freedom to read and learn what she wanted, she was troubled by how others lived. Victoria felt sorry for herself because she was lonely and controlled, but her tours made her learn to feel for others who had it much worse. The teen queen would spend her life trying to make life easier for those who had little.

FAST FACT

Queen Victoria admired the gypsies. Gypsies are a group of nomadic people with eastern European roots. They are known for traveling from place to place and keeping to themselves. Some gypsies practiced fortune telling or other carnival-like lifestyles. English society saw gypsies as dirty criminals who could not be trusted, but Victoria did not. She loved that they had the freedom to travel wherever they wanted, and that they had strong families who watched out for one another. She once wrote how beautiful she found their little children.

The people of England were captivated by the teenage Victoria. She had grown from a round, stubborn toddler into a slender young woman with large, bright eyes and a creamy, rosebud complexion. Victoria was honest and confident with a strong sense of duty and honor.

Soon, captains, dukes, and princes were claiming to be in love with the soon-to-be queen. Every social engagement on her calendar seemed to have men both young and old who were interested in marrying her. None of these felt right to Victoria, and she was lucky she had her protective and ambitious mother to hold them all at bay. The teenager was not interested in marriage now that she would be free from being told what to do as soon as she became queen.

Victoria became so popular that the king became frustrated with her mother and John Conroy for parading her around like a show horse. He refused to speak directly to them or invite them to events. King William IV had a good relationship with Victoria, though, and spent what time he could with her visiting and talking about royal life and the possibilities of her future.

CHAPTER THREE

"I Shall Not Fail"

The year 1837 felt magical for Victoria because she would turn 18. She was now old enough to be queen, if the time came, without the interference of her mother or John Conroy. Her uncle, King William IV, was in poor health. He continued to decline, and by early summer, was in such a bad state that everyone at Kensington Palace was on pins and needles, knowing Victoria could become ruler at any hour.

In the early morning hours of June 20, 1837, two important men arrived at the gates of Kensington Palace before Victoria had awakened for the day. The Archbishop of Canterbury and Lord Conyngham, the King's **chamberlain**, brought news that would change her life forever.

When the news reached Kensington Palace, the gates were still locked. The men were let in but made to wait an hour until Victoria's mother would wake her up. Upon hearing the news, Victoria did not bother to put on a fashionable pretty gown, but slipped on her house shoes and followed her mother down.

The duchess shook Victoria awake and helped her dress in morning robes, then they smoothed down her hair. The independent young woman immediately set the example for how she would rule with a mother over her shoulder: she asked the duchess to remain with her governess outside the room where the officials waited. Victoria then closed the door on them both to meet with the men alone.

As Lehzen waited outside Victoria's room, the officials entered and dropped to their knees before the young woman. Victoria remained calm when they informed her that King William had passed away during the night, and she was now Queen of the United Kingdom.

Victoria was formally told of her uncle's death and given his death certificate. After accepting the news and congratulations, she stepped outside and cried on her mother's shoulder. It had been over 200 years since the last ruling queen, Queen Elizabeth I, had served England.

In this painting, two officials tell the now-Queen Victoria that
her uncle had passed in the night.

Victoria asked for her new private secretary, Christian Friedrich Stockmar. He was a doctor and a close family friend to Uncle Leopold, who had recommended him. She then met with the country's prime minister for the first official time as queen.

One of the greatest influences on Victoria in her early years as queen was her first prime minister, Lord Melbourne. The prime minister was thoughtful and slow to rush to judgment, but he also understood the importance of discipline. His thoughtful counsel and discussions with Queen Victoria helped ease her into the political world of Parliament. It also made him a most trusted friend and advisor.

Almost immediately after accepting the responsibility to serve as queen and meeting her prime minister, Victoria had to report to the Privy Council. Determined to face them alone, she asked Lord Melbourne to remain outside.

The new queen greeted the council members kindly and even stopped to kiss the cheek of the Duke of Sussex, who was too old to bow to kiss her hand. She read a declaration to accept her calling in a confident voice, and it made a delightful impression on them all.

Soon, Queen Victoria was on her way to learning how to work with Parliament to run a country. Her lonely childhood prepared her to be an independent thinker and rely on her instincts. The public fell in love with her youth, beauty, and charm.

CORONATION

A king or queen receives a crown during a special ceremony called a **coronation**. Victoria's coronation did not happen right away, but a little over a year after her uncle died. This was because coronations were not scheduled while the country was mourning for the last king or queen. Traditionally, coronations are not scheduled for months, even up to a year, after the death of an English monarch. Victoria was still the acting monarch of the United Kingdom, however.

One of the first things Victoria did when she became queen was order her mother out of the bedroom they shared. The duchess was moved to a different part of the house. Next, Victoria ordered John Conroy out of Kensington Palace and away from her mother. She decided to change addresses, too. Within a month of her uncle's death, she sent word for **Buckingham Palace** in London to be renovated so that she could move in.

Buckingham Palace was built in 1703 for a duke and bought by King George III in 1761. It was in pretty bad shape when Victoria decided she wanted to live there. It was bigger than Kensington Palace, but even once it was repaired, the old place still leaked and suffered from smoking chimneys. It was not protected by an enormous park like Kensington, which meant there were more people and pollution from the coal wafting in from all of the homes and factory chimneys.

FAST FACT

There have been many different royal residences in England's history. When Victoria became queen, she not only had the option of living at Kensington Palace, but St. James Palace, Buckingham Palace, Windsor Palace, or Holyrood House in Scotland.

The official coronation for Queen Victoria, the moment when she would receive her crown, was scheduled for June 27, 1838. It would be one great party for the people of the United Kingdom who had not been in love with a royal for many years. No one had been fond of her uncles. As princes, they had lived for money, fashion, and entertainment instead of turning their attention to the people. Now, there was hope Victoria would be different. This meant carnivals, food, drinking, and dancing all over London and out in the country sides of Wales, Ireland, and Scotland, all in Queen Victoria's honor. People came from all over the country. So many crowded into London hoping to get a glimpse of the young queen that it seemed, as Charles Dickens reported, "the world was alive with men."[12]

At 10 o'clock in the morning, Queen Victoria left Buckingham Palace by carriage, dressed in a red velvet dress. The ride to **Westminster Abbey**, London's royal church, was only three miles away, but it would take almost two hours to get there because of the huge crowds. As trumpets blared and guns were shot in loud salutes, Victoria added scarlet and fur-trimmed robes for the ceremony in the abbey. She entered with eight young girls in silver and white trailing behind her in a somber procession.

The coronation lasted five hours. The new queen had to remove her robes and put on a white **tunic** and simple tiara. There were prayers and oils dripped onto her head. When her red robe was put back across her shoulders, a scepter was put in her hand and a ruby ring forced onto her ring finger.

FAST FACT

The 21-gun salute began as an English naval tradition to announce authority. It eventually became a custom for other celebrations. A 41-gun salute is given for a royal event.

12. Baird, Julia. 2017.

When the glittering crown was finally placed on her head, Victoria was officially the Queen of the United Kingdom. The official 41 cannons fired, trumpets blew, and drums sounded as the people cheered and cried.

Queen Victoria poses for her official coronation portrait.

FAST FACT

The royal crown placed on Victoria's head, called the Imperial State Crown, is still used today. It features over 2,900 diamonds, sapphires, rubies, and pearls around a purple velvet cap. The cap and jewels are mounted onto a crown frame made of gold, silver, and platinum.

The people of the United Kingdom celebrated for days, but the new queen did not. When Victoria returned from the coronation, the first thing she did was call for her dog, Dash. As the world celebrated a new English monarch, the little queen gave her pet a bath.

FIRST DUTIES AND MISTAKES

Victoria loved being queen because she could make her own choices about everything. It was a busy new life full of banquets, balls, meetings, reports, and a great deal of letter writing. She wrote so much and so often, her work today fills volumes of books in England's historical archives!

FAST FACT

It is estimated that Victoria wrote an average of 2,500 words a day by hand.[13]
There were no keyboards and computers in 1837.

It wasn't long before politicians and newspapers understood that she had a strong will and mind of her own. If she did not agree with a politician or problem brought before her, she would make up her own mind or create a different solution.

The young queen wouldn't even follow the rules for royal manners if she did not like them. At dinner parties, she would not allow men to disappear to drink and smoke as was the custom, at least not for very long. She also chose to ride a horse to some events when she was expected to ride in the royal carriage. Victoria behaved how she believed was proper and fair and expected those around her to do so, too.

13. Lloyd, Ian. 2014.

The queen became so close to her prime minister, Lord Melbourne, in the first few years of her reign that many people thought that she was in love with him. The pair spent time together almost every day working on the affairs of the United Kingdom, and she adored his company. She often wrote how much she loved him as a father and friend, and how she trusted his knowledge and cherished their time together.

Lord Melbourne, a faithful friend to Victoria, poses here for a portrait.

Lord Melbourne was a widower, but he was much older than the teenage queen. He had been married for a time to a beautiful woman and had a son, but the marriage failed and his wife eventually died. Although it was scandalous for a man whose wife had left him to serve so high in the government at the time, Lord Melbourne continued to serve in Parliament. He became prime minister for the first time in 1834, three years before Victoria became queen.

Although she had the support of the prime minister and the people, Queen Victoria was still a young girl in many ways, and she made mistakes in the early years of her reign. Some of them were considered scandalous and stuck in the memories of those who would carry on her legacy.

Lady Flora

Lady Flora Hastings was a single woman who served as a lady-in-waiting to Victoria's mother, the Duchess of Kent. In May of 1839, almost a year after the coronation, Victoria noticed that Lady Flora did not seem to feel well and that her stomach looked round.

Lady Flora was a trusted friend of the duchess and John Conroy. The public liked her and would cheer when she was announced. These things made Victoria uneasy. It would be a scandal if Lady Flora were to have a baby and not be married. She asked Lady Flora's doctor about it, and learned the lady-in-waiting was having stomach pain and taking medicine.

Victoria did not trust Conroy and her mother so much that she stubbornly decided that Lady Flora was going to have a baby after all. She asked Dr. Clark to spy on Lady Flora and then accused her of being pregnant. Lady Flora promised it was not true and that she was just sick. Victoria didn't believe poor Flora. She ordered her to undergo a medical examination. Even though it was painful and humiliating, she had a checkup. Dr. Clark agreed that she was not pregnant after all, but suffered from some kind of stomach or organ illness.

The public was angry about Victoria's accusations. The newspapers printed all kinds of stories. Some said Lady Flora was going to have a baby, and others accused Victoria of being cruel and immature. Some thought it was political since Queen Victoria was a Whig and Lady Flora was from a strong Tory family. Even Lord Melbourne was attacked as prime minister because he did nothing to stop the rumors or Victoria's behavior.

Lady Flora grew sicker and weaker. Victoria was sorry for her mistake and went to visit her but found her close to dying. The lady-in-waiting was actually a shy and kind woman who had devoted herself to the duchess for many years. Flora died on the fifth of July, only a couple months after Victoria's accusations. The public was so angry with Queen Victoria during this time they booed and hissed when they saw the royal carriage.

The Bedchamber Crisis

The newspapers reported on the **Bedchamber Crisis** around the same time as Lady Flora's scandal. A queen had assistants who helped her in her personal life and also on special occasions. These helpers were called **Ladies of the Bedchamber**, although they did not actually stay or work in the queen's bedroom.

Traditionally, Ladies of the Bedchamber were aristocrats or relatives of the queen. Queen Victoria's ladies were Whigs, like Victoria's family, but in 1839 the Whigs lost power in Parliament. The Tories were now in power, and so two things happened that made stubborn Victoria dig in her heels.

First, her friend and prime minister, Lord Melbourne, quit because his party was no longer in power. The young queen was so upset, she cried for days. She wrote him letters begging him to at least visit her. When they met together, she sobbed, "You will not forsake me!"[14] He promised her he would not and encouraged her to work with the new party's leader. She refused.

The second event that created the crisis was the new prime minister, Sir Robert Peel. He insisted that Queen Victoria pick new **Ladies of the Bedchamber** who were Tories, just like the ruling party in Parliament.

FAST FACT

There are actually two Bedchamber titles for those who assist a queen. They are usually called Ladies-in-Waiting. A queen has a personal secretary to help her with business, but she also has the Ladies of the Bedchamber for social events, ceremonies, and other public occasions. Besides the Ladies of the Bedchamber, there are the Women of the Bedchamber. The Women of the Bedchamber assist the queen on a daily basis, usually with bathing and dressing.

Victoria refused to obey the new prime minister's wishes. She felt like he was trying to control her, just like her mother and John Conroy had done when she was a child. In her diary, she wrote that she told him, "I could not give up any of my ladies!"[15]

The new monarch

A king or queen was not supposed to take sides in parliamentary politics, no matter what party they liked, so Sir Robert Peel, as well as the people of England, thought Victoria was playing favorites. Even though the newspapers wrote about her stubbornness, she would not give in to Sir Robert Peels' demands.

14. Baird, Julia. 2017
15. Baird, Julia. 2017

The new prime minister grew so frustrated dealing with the queen's strong opinions and refusal to work with him that he quit. Lord Melbourne was made prime minister again, and the Tories and the public became very critical of the queen's interference.

Sir Robert Peel poses here for his official portrait.

Victoria did not mind it too much. She was thrilled to be able to work with Lord Melbourne again.

FAST FACT

Since the time of Queen Victoria, the United Kingdom has been a constitutional monarchy. The king or queen is the Head of State, but does not make laws or other decisions. That's Parliament's job. Parliament is a governing body of aristocrats and elected officials that are ruled by the party that wins each general election.

Victoria came from a strong, traditional Tory family that believed in a monarch's power over Parliament, but her feelings would later change as she matured. At the beginning of her reign as queen, she spent up to six hours a day with Lord Melbourne who acted both as her minister and almost as a personal secretary. Melbourne taught Victoria about his political views on history and religion. He also encouraged her to be self-confident and taught her to stand up for herself as a monarch.

The prime minister himself did not accomplish much politically while tutoring Queen Victoria. Many people felt he was so concerned about her personal life and happiness that he failed to educate her on problems with the poor and opportunities for education. During Victoria's unpopularity during the Flora Hastings scandal and the Bedchamber Crisis, he refused to criticize or correct her. In some ways, Victoria's first prime minister built up a sense of power and entitlement that she needed, but for the people of the United Kingdom, especially the poor, it came at a high price.

Young Victoria did not accomplish much politically as a new queen. It would take a few years of study, experience, and the influence of a German prince named Albert to help her mature as a monarch.

CHAPTER FOUR

Handsome Prince Albert

In 1836, a year before Victoria would become queen, **Prince Albert of Saxe-Coburg** made his first official visit to his cousin, Victoria. They were the same age and first cousins. Uncle Leopold made it no secret he thought the future queen and her German cousin would make a great match. Victoria, however, was not interested. She had a country to worry about and looked forward to not being told what to do.

That spring, Albert and his older brother, Earnest, visited Kensington to meet Victoria and celebrate her 17th birthday. The three cousins had a good time together. She loved visitors, and the future queen decided she adored these cousins who were friendly, happy, and ready to have fun.

Albert, Victoria decided, had a beautiful nose and eyes. She even found his mouth pretty enough to write about in her diary. Unfortunately, while he had the striking beauty Victoria always wished for, he did not have her strength. The future husband of Queen Victoria struggled with stomach and other health problems his entire life. This often made him appear pale and weak. Victoria wrote to her uncle that she admired her cousin a great deal, but he fell so sick during his first visit to Victoria that she was not impressed. Not on that visit anyway.

AN AWKWARD PROPOSAL

Victoria and Albert stayed in touch after they met the first time in 1836. They wrote letters full of friendliness and encouragement, while their families continued to pressure them to get together. Victoria made it clear she was not interested in a relationship, while Albert remained polite but impatient with her indecision. She told her Uncle Leopold that when it came to marriage, "I have no anxiety for such an event."[16]

Albert did not mind if she did not marry him, but he wasn't interested in waiting around either. He told a family member he did not find her that beautiful, but liked that she was kind and smart. Things changed quickly three years later.

In October of 1839, Albert and his brother, Ernest, traveled to London to visit their cousin again.

When Victoria saw her cousins on the palace steps, she was struck with a sudden shyness when she saw how much Albert had changed. The thin, pale boy had grown up. Although a little seasick, Albert stood almost six feet tall with dark, trim mustache. Victoria later wrote in her diary that she felt smitten. "My heart is quite going,"[17] she admitted.

It may not have been love at first sight, but in the end it was love at second sight, and it lasted a lifetime. The couple spent as much time together as they could for days, spending their time walking, chatting, dining, and dancing. Victoria adored Albert's kindness and sensibility. He enjoyed her company and her intelligence.

---

16. Baird, Julia 2017
17. Baird, Julia 2017

People thought the two of them had quite different personalities. Victoria liked to go to balls and sleep late. Albert liked to wake up early, take walks, hunt, read, and study. He once found Victoria's lifestyle a little too wild for his taste, but her outgoing, cheerful personality struck something inside of him that made him see her only as charming and adorable.

A PRIVATE MEETING

Only a matter of days passed before Victoria changed her mind about marriage. She was madly in love. A marriage to Albert would make her uncle and mother very happy, too. However, there was one big problem: she couldn't expect for him to ask her to marry him — he couldn't!

It was traditional for a man to ask a woman to marry in England during this era. Because Victoria was queen, every man was beneath her, even the ones she admired and loved. The only way she would ever marry was to ask a man herself. Victoria made up her mind, and once her mind was set she did not hesitate or change it. It would be a most awkward proposal, but it was the only way to marry the man she wanted to be with the rest of her life.

On October 15, 1839, only days after Albert's arrival, Victoria sent a note asking him to meet with her privately. He'd been out hunting, but he hurried to see her within an hour of his return. Struck again with shyness and trembling with nerves, Victoria managed an awkward proposal of marriage not knowing if he would laugh or say yes. Rather than ask him outright, Victoria hinted around until he understood and agreed.

She explained what happened in her diary: *"I said to him that I thought he must be aware of why I wished him to come and that it would make me too happy if would consent to what I wished."*[18]

---

18. Baird, Julia. 2017

Luckily for Victoria, Albert had fallen for her, too. He understood it would unite their families and please Uncle Leopold. Most of all, Albert wanted a family full of love and children. His parents' marriage did not last, and he was separated from his mother at a young age. She died in 1831 at 30 years old. He was never close to his father, either.

Albert was so confident Victoria was the woman he should marry, he wrote a letter to his grandmother. He gushed about how he loved her outgoing, open personality and that he felt they'd work well together. He just knew that "we shall be happy together.[19]" It wouldn't be easy. His wife would be queen, and he would be one of her subjects.

Victoria kept the engagement a secret from her mother for almost a month. When the Duchess of Kent heard the news, she cried with happiness. The newspapers in England did not. They didn't want another German in the palace, and they didn't think it was good for cousins to marry. Some articles called Albert a "puppet." Others complained he was too young and that he was too poor for a prince. It seemed almost everyone felt he did not have any government experience and would be of no use to the kingdom.

They were wrong.

A WEDDING AT ST. JAMES

Victoria married her German prince on February 10, 1840. Only four months had passed since Albert had come for his second visit to see his cousin. Some people thought it was a very short engagement, but Victoria did not care. She was ready to be wed to her closest friend who had also stolen her heart.

---

19. Baird, Julia. 2017

Queen Victoria wore traditional wedding garb to marry Prince Albert.

The queen left Buckingham Palace for the Chapel Royal of St. James Palace on the morning of her wedding day and traveled in an elegant coach through streets that were so crowded people fell from trees where they had climbed up for a view. There were gun salutes and trumpets. Those who had hissed at her for her earlier mistakes now cheered with delight. Vendors sold trinkets and souvenirs with Victoria's face painted on them. Even though it was rainy and windy, everyone wanted to see the queen and celebrate, just like they did during her coronation ceremony.

When Victoria stepped from her carriage, everyone fell in love with the sweet, nervous bride. She wore a white silk dress with white lace, diamond earrings, and a crown of white blossoms and green-colored orange blossom leaves.

The bride's wedding party included 12 young girls to carry the queen's 18-foot long, white train that billowed behind her gown. Her bedchamber ladies and women were with her, too. Once inside the chapel, Victoria found Prince Albert waiting for her in a bright red uniform. The **Order of the Garter**, a star-shaped medal with a red cross in the center, was pinned to his chest.

FAST FACT

Because of the cost of buying a new gown, most brides wore colored wedding dresses in the early 19th century. It made sense to have a dress to wear for later occasions that wouldn't stain. Victoria chose white because it showed the lovely lace she had ordered from lace makers in Devon, England. She hoped that her white silk dress and lace would help the fabric and lace industries. It worked for a time, and the skilled workers had plenty of orders and a new trend.

This portrait was engraved upon Queen Victoria and Prince Albert's return from their marriage service at St. James' palace.

The couple exchanged promises to love and be faithful to each other until they died. People noticed that Victoria had refused to remove the word "obey" from her vows, although she could have because she was queen. Cheers erupted once more as the couple left the chapel for their carriage. There would be a great feast, and then they would travel several hours away to Windsor Castle to be alone. Victoria later wrote, "This was the happiest day of my life."[20]

CHILDREN IN THE PALACE

When Queen Victoria was a teenager, she not only thought she did not want to get married for a long time, she didn't look forward to having children, either. It often comes as a big surprise to people that this decided, independent woman had so many children in a span of 20 years —and that they all lived.

FAST FACT

In 1800, 43 percent of the world's newborns died before their 5th birthday.[21]

After their wedding, Victoria and Albert returned to live at Buckingham Palace. Before too long, their first child came along. Victoria surprised everyone by staying healthy and strong while she was pregnant. She still exercised and went to parties. It seemed nothing could slow her down.

The couple stayed close even though many people thought Victoria would lose interest in working with Parliament and her prime minister. Although he was not the ruling monarch, Albert began to help with Victoria's official duties.

20. Baird, Julia. 2017
21. Roser, Max. 2017

When it came time for Victoria to have the baby, Albert stayed with her the entire time. This was unusual, but it set the pattern for Albert's caring interest in his family and his involvement as a father.

A baby girl was born on November 21, 1840, and they named her Victoria after her mother. Later, the new princess was officially christened Victoria Adelaide Mary Louise. Victoria wasn't sure about motherhood at first; she thought all babies looked like frogs, but she adored her children and loved to play and care for them.

Although the queen did not want children right away, she had another baby a year later. Albert Edward was born on November 9, 1841. The boy, nicknamed "Bertie," would grow up to inherit the crown after his mother died.

Victoria and Albert had five girls and four boys. After their second child, Prince Edward, was born, to everyone's surprise, seven more children joined the royal family. The children of Queen Victoria would go on to marry dukes, princes, princesses, and aristocrats of several European nations.

This photograph of Queen Victoria and Prince Albert with their children was given to the National Portrait Gallery in London in 1977.

FAST FACT

The children born to Queen Victoria and Prince Albert were:

1. Princess Victoria; "Vicky"
   Birth: November 21, 1840
   Death: August 5, 1901.
   Marriage: Frederick III, German Emperor

Victoria, Princess Royal, became Crown
Princess of Prussia in 1867.

2. Prince Albert Edward, Prince of Wales; "Bertie"
   Birth: 1841
   Death: 1910
   Marriage: Princess Alexandra of Denmark

Prince of Wales Albert Edward, the future king
of England, poses here wearing the uniform of
the admiral.

3. Princess Alice
   Birth: 1843
   Death: 1878
   Marriage: Prince Louis of Hesse

Princess Alice is portrayed here in the dress
she wore at her first Drawing Room.

4. Prince Alfred
   Birth: 1844
   Death: 1900
   Marriage: Grand-Duchess Marie
   Alexandrovna

Prince Alfred was 8 years old when this portrait of him was drawn.

5. Princess Helena
   Birth: 1846
   Death: 1923
   Marriage: Prince Christian of
   Schleswig-Holstein

Princess Helena married Prince Christian of Schleswig-Holstein when she was 20 years old.

6. Princess Louise
   Birth: 1848
   Death: 1939
   Marriage: John, Marquess of Lorne

This photograph was taken of Princess Louise, Queen Victoria's rebellious daughter, in Venice.

7. Prince Arthur
   Birth: 1850
   Death: 1942
   Marriage: Princess Louise of Prussia

Pictured here, Prince Arthur's full title is Duke of Connaught and Strathearn.

8. Prince Leopold
   Birth: 1853
   Death: 1884
   Marriage: Princess Helena of Waldeck and Pyrmont

Prince Leopold was only 8 years old when his father, Prince Albert, died. Here he is with his mother, both dressed in mourning attire.

9. Princess Beatrice
   Birth: 1857
   Death: 1944
   Marriage: Prince Henry of Battenberg

Queen Victoria is pictured here with her youngest daughter, Princess Beatrice.

Even as Victoria ruled as queen, she was a part of her children's everyday lives. They were the first children born at Buckingham Palace. They filled the halls with games and laughter. She made sure each one of them received a good education, including her daughters.

During this time, Victoria grew closer to her own mother, the Duchess of Kent. Albert encouraged the queen to make things right with their children's grandmother. The Duchess spent time with them, helped raise them, and had a good relationship with Victoria until she died in 1861.

FAST FACT

Even the queen made clumsy mistakes, just like everybody else. In 1890, a women's magazine reported that Queen Victoria accidentally burned a handful of pearls she had been saving for her daughters. Pearls were expensive jewels. At that time, just three could cost up to £500. To be frugal, Victoria had been buying just a few at a time every year so she could make pearl necklaces for her daughters' weddings. However, on her last purchase, Victoria left them wrapped in tissue on her desk. She later picked them up and threw them into the fire, thinking they were trash. The pearls could not be recovered or found in the fireplace. After contacting her jeweler, she learned the hard way that pearls burn easily into ashes.

Before the family grew so large, Albert realized there was a big drawback to living in the city. The children would have no forests or streams to play in. He and Victoria realized the family needed a place to get fresh air, run about, and have privacy. After traveling around, the couple decided to buy **Osbourne House** in the Isle of Wight.

Osbourne House rested near the shores of the Isle of Wight, an island in the English Channel. It is close to the southern coast of England and has beautiful rocky land and beaches. Victoria thought it so beautiful she proclaimed, "It is impossible to imagine a prettier spot!"[22]

Victoria and Albert had the ancient house rebuilt with private rooms, towers, and gardens. A special cottage was built on the grounds so that the children could learn homemaking skills and how to take care of themselves without a servant. Osbourne House was a special getaway for the royal family, and they loved it very much.

FAST FACT

Today Osbourne House is open for tours. The giant home is decorated with things just as Victoria and Albert liked it. Besides the beautiful paintings and furniture, there are special artifacts and other art on display. Nearby is Princess Victoria Beach. This was a private beach where the queen could get in the water and where her children learned to swim.

After her second baby, Victoria and Albert first traveled north into Scotland to an ancient, ivy-covered castle called **Balmoral**. They fell in love with the quietness, endless views, and friendly people. As their family grew, it became a second home for the family.

With three light-colored stone stories and two towers, Balmoral Castle was a special place where Albert could hike for miles, hunt, and fish without having to run into strangers or fans. Victoria loved to draw, walk, and mingle with the local people who were friendly and laid back.

Eventually, the queen and her husband even wore the traditional Scottish plaid, called **tartan**. There were dinners and dancing in the evenings and

---

22. English-heritage.org.uk

many special guests visited them there. Years later in her old age, Victoria fondly said that Balmoral Castle was where she felt the happiest in her life.

FAST FACT

The northwest part of Scotland is called the Highlands, and highlanders are famous for their tartan. Tartan is a rough, cotton fabric made from Scottish wool that is plaid, or crisscrossed, in all sorts of bright colors like blue, green, yellow, and red. Each tartan represents a Scottish clan, or family group. Balmoral patterns were purple and gray.

The people of the United Kingdom and in many other countries loved that Victoria and Albert had a large, close family. The public romanticized life in the royal household but in reality, the queen's family was not without its problems. Victoria loved her children, but like every family, there were ups and downs as the children grew into adulthood. Some made Victoria and Albert very proud; others, like Prince Bertie, had his share of scandals that embarrassed the family.

In her later years, Victoria had a hard time letting go of her children once they married, but she always made sure to have some of her daughters close by. After her husband died, the queen insisted her daughters lived near her. Beatrice, her youngest daughter, was not allowed to marry unless she promised to continue living with her mother.

Victoria was not just content raising her children; she was at her happiest in the years she was married to Albert. Besides their very different personalities, they had different roles, too. Victoria's job was to reign over the United Kingdom; Albert's job would be to act as husband to the queen and father to his children. He would do both with kindness, cleverness, and determination — until it was acceptable for him to do more.

A STRONG PARTNERSHIP

Once married, Victoria spent the majority of the next three decades having children and raising them to adulthood. She always struggled with the conflict of her two very different roles as queen and mother. When Albert and Victoria first married, she insisted she would rule alone, but by the time the second child came along, she realized Albert was just as capable making wise decisions. Together, they could rule as a team.

Albert wanted to do more, but he focused on helping and playing with the children in the early years. Victoria picked flowers with them and taught them their prayers. Albert took them on trips to zoos and museums.

Although it worked, the marriage in the royal household wasn't perfect. At first, the newlywed couple found that they argued quite a bit. Victoria had a fast temper and would shout and stomp. Albert's quiet nature led him to ignore his wife or hide behind locked doors. It was usually Victoria who broke the stalemate. If pounding on Albert's door didn't work, she resolved their conflicts with apologies, handwritten notes, and sorrow for her terrible temper. Fortunately, the queen loved as passionately as she fought.

Soon, Albert began to take over some of Victoria's everyday tasks like blotting, or stamping, her signature on paperwork. They eventually pushed two desks together and worked side by side. Sometimes, Victoria felt so busy with her children that she permitted Albert to attend some of her meetings with government officials.

Not everyone thought Albert filling in was a good idea. He was still a German foreigner and had to prove himself. He could never be king, not officially, but he won the hearts of Englishmen one step at a time.

This photograph of Queen Victoria and Prince Albert was
taken by photographer Roger Fenton in 1854.

Besides going to public ceremonies with and without Victoria, Albert made
a special effort to focus on important issues of the day. While he understood that his marriage to the queen was his official career, he wanted people to see that he cared about the country and could, and would, fight for
positive changes. He later became thought of as equal to Victoria because
of his dedication to their work.

Victoria was always proud of Albert no matter what he set his mind out to
do. They had close to an equal marriage compared to most marriages of the
time. In 1857, Victoria gave Albert the title of "Prince Regent." This meant
he could rule as a monarch in the event of the queen's illness or absence.
Albert worked hard the rest of his life supporting his family and guiding
the affairs of the kingdom.

CHAPTER FIVE

Victoria Rules

Victoria did not make or enforce the laws of her country, as the United Kingdom was a **constitutional monarchy**. As queen, Victoria met and worked with Parliament through her prime ministers. Parliament made the laws, but the queen expressed her opinions about them and urged her supporters to vote her way.

If she admired her prime minister, or "PM", Victoria was easy to work with and a great deal was accomplished. If she did not, she was stubborn and pressed her opinions and judgments on her advisors to get what she wanted. The young queen didn't always win, but many leaders criticized her for putting her nose too deep into Parliament's business when she was supposed to remain neutral.

These smooth and rough periods meant sometimes things ran well between the queen and her PM, and sometimes things took a disastrous turn. Some of the ministers understood how to flatter her and engage her to work as a team. Others tried to out-influence her or were so different from her that she simply found them annoying.

FAST FACT

The Whig or Tory leader who won the most seats in Parliament after an election is appointed Prime Minister by the queen.

Queen Victoria had nine prime ministers during her reign that served multiple times. She did not always want a certain candidate to be prime minister, but to be fair, she had to approve Parliament's choice.

PRIME MINISTERS OF QUEEN VICTORIA

1. Lord Melbourne (William Lamb) 1835-1841

2. Sir Robert Peel (1841-1846)

3. Lord John Russell (1846-1852)

4. The Earl of Derby (Edward Smith-Stanley)

5. The Earl of Aberdeen (George Hamilton-Gordon) 1852-1855

6. Viscount Palmerston Henry John Temple (1855-1855

7. Lord John Russell 1865-1866

8. Benjamin Disraeli 1868

9. William Ewart Gladstone 1868-1874

10. Marquess of Salisbury Robert Gascoyne-Cecil 1885-1886

11. Earl of Rosebery Archibald Primrose 1894-1895

Victoria never grew as close to any other prime minister as she did her first advisor, Lord Melbourne. Besides a rough patch with Sir Robert Peel, she later worked well with Prime Minister Benjamin Disraeli.

Disraeli was a charming man. Tall, thin, and always impeccably dressed, Disraeli surprised Parliament by becoming the first Jewish prime minister. He knew how to charm women, and Queen Victoria was not immune. They worked together on social reform and relations with Russia after Victoria was widowed, and they got along quite well.

FAST FACT

Benjamin Disraeli was not only a successful politician who served twice as Prime Minister, but he was a novelist, too. He once said, "The secret of success in life is for a man to be ready for his opportunity when it comes."

Disraeli called Victoria his "faery queen." After his wife died, he said to a friend that Queen Victoria was the "only person in this world left to me that I do love."[23]

Queen Victoria and Prime Minister Disraeli
walk closely together in this sketch.

23. Baird, Julia 2017

One of Victoria's greatest antagonists chosen to work with her was William Gladstone. He served as prime minister four different times. Gladstone had Scottish roots. He'd gone to school and chosen the Church of England for a career, but his father talked him out of it, and he realized his strong, confident opinions were a good fit for politics.

Gladstone served with Sir Robert Peel in the Treasury, and his conservative views propelled him forward in a time of conflict between the two parties. Many people did not trust Gladstone, including the queen, because many of his closest friends were Catholic, and he believed Ireland should be free to rule itself.

FAST FACT

Ireland became part of the United Kingdom in 1801 and was ruled by Parliament in London. By the 1870s, some Irish and English politicians began fighting for Irish Home Rule, a movement that caused violence and a split in the Liberal party. It took four bills and another 50 years before the Government of Ireland Act of 1920 passed, and two different parliaments were formed in the north and the south of Ireland. Today, Northern Ireland is still a part of the United Kingdom. The south of Ireland is called the Republic of Ireland.

Victoria complained that Gladstone was arrogant and stubborn, as well as a tyrant. She called him a "ridiculous, wild, and incomprehensible old fanatic."[24] Even when he became quite ill, she could not bring herself to be kind or apologize to him when she visited. He once said Queen Victoria was "enough to kill any man."[25]

---

24. Hibbert, Christopher. 2011
25. Baird, Julia. 2017

ALBERT'S INFLUENCE

Prince Albert also had a great impact on Victoria's opinions and policies. Anything he felt strongly about, she came to care about, too. Some of Albert's causes included abolishing slavery around the world, tackling poverty and poor health, and advancing scientific advancements.

One of Albert's most striking public speaking events was on June 1, 1840, at Exeter Hall in defense of human rights. At the time, he was President of the African Civilisation Society for the extinction of the slave trade. During his speech, which he wrote, he said to the 4,500 persons present:

"I have been induced to preside at the meeting of this Society from a conviction of its paramount importance to the great interests of humanity and justice. I deeply regret that the benevolent and perservering exersions of England to abolish that atrocious traffic in human beings have not led to a satisfactory conclusion. I sincerely trust that this great county will not relax in its efforts until it has finally and forever put an end to that state of things so repugnant to the principles of Christianity and to the best feelings of our nature...."[26]

Prince Albert also educated Victoria on poverty and exposed her to the real life of those struggling to survive. He became the champion of the poor. Albert was horrified that the pitiful face of poverty seemed to be everywhere in his new adopted country.

With his wife's approval, the prince became president of the Society for Improving the Condition of the Labour Classes. He rounded up charitable donations from the rich. In 1846, he managed the construction of new homes, with improved sanitation and ventilation, in north London. He

---

26. Albert, Prince. 1840

also tried to improve the welfare system for those who had nothing. Albert shared his goals with all who would listen. His dreams were to improve education for children, job training for adults, healthy living conditions, and make available grants and savings for those who needed them.

Prince Albert is wearing the Golden Fleece in this portrait by
Franz Xaver Winterhalter, 1842.

The prince loved science and new technologies. He was a great thinker and shared his excitement with his wife, who could be slow to come aboard. One interesting fact about Prince Albert is that he loved the railroad and encouraged the use and popularity of steam engines. In fact, during the summer of 1842, Albert talked Victoria into riding on a steam engine-powered train on a railway. She liked it so much that she had her own royal train cars for the rest of her life.

THE GREAT EXHIBITION

One of the most celebrated events of Victoria's reign was the **Great Exhibition of 1851**, but the surprising truth is that it was Albert's idea, and he did most of the work.

Albert wanted to have a fair displaying all of the new sciences and technologies from around the world, as well as plants, animals, and other things rare to an everyday Englishman. Queen Victoria agreed, and together they put on one of the most exciting exhibits that the world had ever seen. Today, it is considered the first official World's Fair.

FAST FACT

The World's Fair is a worldwide exposition that displays inventions, art, and other achievements from countries around the world. The last World's Fair was held in Astana, Kazakhstan, in 2017.

To house the many inventions and artifacts, a giant glass building was designed. Using cast iron frames, glass windows were inserted to let in light, making it look like a giant conservatory. It was called the Glass Palace. Albert wanted it to be a symbol of the beauty and originality of modern science. The construction took seven months and required 2,000 men to get it finished in time.

Once it was finished, the newspapers and many aristocrats declared it ugly and tacky. The people loved it though, and everyone was excited. One peculiar problem did arise: as soon as the Glass Palace was finished, organizers realized that all of the sparrows around London would stain the pretty windows with their bird droppings, so hawks were brought in to chase them out. It worked.

The Great Exhibition opened on May 1, 1851. England reserved half of the space, and the rest was filled up by over 15,000 contributions from places like Germany, France, Russia, India, Canada, and the United States. There were about 100,000 things to see; so much that it couldn't be done in one day. Thousands of people attended, even Queen Victoria. She enjoyed it and went several times. Visitors were able to see marvelous inventions and new products from all around the world.

FAST FACT

Here is a sample of some of the exhibits displayed at the fair:

a massive hydraulic press	carriages
a steam-hammer	bicycles
adding machines	printing presses
a sportsman's knife	textile machines
a printing machine	agricultural machines
a cigarette folding machine	locomotives
folding pianos	a fire engine

carved ivory	tapestries
gold and gemstones	porcelain
a stuffed elephant	vases and urns
Colt's repeating fire-arms	furs
McCormick's reaping machine	watches
silks	toys

The Great Exhibition lasted for six months and welcomed millions of visitors. In the end, it was considered a smashing success. The Glass Palace was moved to Hyde Park afterward, but unfortunately, the conservatory burned down in 1936.

VICTORIA'S FIRST WAR

When Queen Victoria turned 34 years old in 1853, she had ruled the United Kingdom for over a decade. England had enjoyed years of peace, but Europe and the powers at each country's head were jockeying for position and power.

One concern abroad was the country of Russia. It was ruled by a **tsar**, or king, named Nicholas I. Nicholas I was a hard man who lost his father in a revolution. He became king when his brother died and took over the country with an iron hand. He ruled as an **autocrat**, which meant he had absolute power. Some say he froze the progress and development of his land for 30 years.

Turkey was another worry for England. The important country provided land access to Asia and had a port on the Black Sea, which led to the Mediterranean. This meant sea access.

Turkey had grown unstable through crime and persecution. The military was weak, and the state still lived in the past with few modern advancements. Worse, Christians in Turkey were outnumbered by millions of others in different faiths, and were being slaughtered by Muslim extremists.

Both England and France approached Turkey with concern about the safety of Christians in the country, but Russia wanted to sneak into Turkey for its own military and trade uses. The tsar claimed he could protect the Christians better.

That would be a big problem. If Russia were to control Turkey, it could block the English from their routes to India and Asia. The Russians would also have an important seaport and be able to increase the size of their navy. Both advantages worried all of Europe.

England, France, Russia, and Turkey sent letters and leaders back and forth to try to negotiate a solution to the problems. There were a lot of misunderstandings and deliberate ignorance. In the end, Victoria's prime minister sent troops to Turkey's port of **Sevastopol** in the Black Sea while she and Albert were away on holiday. Both of them were furious when they returned, but it was too late.

On October 23, 1853, Turkey declared war on Russia. Since England and Turkey were still allies, Victoria now found her country on the verge of war. The battles became bloody — fast. Four months later, England ordered Russia to remove their troops from the **Danube** region, today's Romania. France chose to stand with England in friendly support. On March 28 of 1854, England declared war on Russia.

The rise of a nightingale

England's military was not any more prepared for war than its young queen. Troops were sent ship by ship, swiftly, but without plans for supplies or first aid. Some men had only swords to defend themselves against Russians with cannons and guns.

FAST FACT

A nightingale is a small, brown bird with a white breast known for its powerful and memorable song.

In the first battles of the war, the United Kingdom lost. Hundreds of men died horrible deaths. The wounded faced just as horrible circumstances. There was no food and little water. No one had made plans for transporting the wounded off the battlefields. No hospitals were set up. This left only the doctors serving aboard the battleships to tend to the dying. Sadly, there were not enough doctors for all of the wounded. Women were not allowed to go to war during that time, even to help care for survivors. There was no one.

FAST FACT

Before the war's end, 23,000 English soldiers would die from wounds and illnesses. Less than 5,000 were killed in action.[27]

Victoria read the horrible reports and cried over the awful stories in the newspapers. She did not know how to conduct a war or how to advise her military leaders. Many people were angry with the government and its lack

---

27. Baird, Julia. 2017

of preparation. Victoria and other aristocrats wrote letters and had fund-raisers in an effort to help.

One person who Victoria would come to know and respect was a woman named **Florence Nightingale**. At first, Victoria did not like to read the newspapers praising Ms. Nightingale's war efforts. Those feelings changed when Victoria realized women acting as nurses could change the outcome of the war.

Henry Herring took this photo of Florence Nightingale circa 1860.

Florence Nightingale was born in Italy in 1820, around the same time as Victoria. She later moved to England with her parents where she received a high degree of education. After helping sick people in her village, the future champion of world health decided to go to nursing school in Germany. When she returned to England, Florence spoke out about the horrible conditions of the wounded soldiers in Crimea.

In 1854, Florence was asked by the Secretary of War to gather up a troop of nurses and travel across the sea to help in the Crimean War effort with 40 other women. There they found the sick and wounded lying in filth and covered in bugs and rats. The nurses set to work teaching the military how to clean and properly care for the wounded. Deaths by disease dropped by two-thirds. Their service and sacrifice changed the way the wounded were cared for in battle and opened the door for women to enter the halls of medicine.

At home, Victoria grieved over the reports of deaths. She wrote letters to soldiers and families. In London, she visited wounded soldiers and spent time talking with them and patting their hands. She really did care, and soon, she became as proud as the people of the work Florence Nightingale was doing for England's soldiers. Florence later met with the queen, and in 1856, Victoria presented her with a brooch for her good deeds and a reward of £250,000.

FAST FACT

The brooch awarded to Florence Nightingale is known as the "Nightingale Jewel." The trailblazing nurse did not spend her reward money on herself; she used it to continue fighting for better health care and conditions.

The Crimean War lasted two and a half years. Russia finally found itself on the losing end when the English decided to lay siege to the harbor and fort. The Russians were trapped for almost a year. Finally, in the fall of 1855, treaties were made between the battling countries, but no one really won. England and France pulled out, and Russia went home.

FAST FACT

The famous poet, Lord Alfred Tennyson wrote a poem about a famous battle in the war that changed the outcome. "The Charge of the Light Brigade" described the charge of over 600 British officers against an entire Russian line. More then two-thirds were killed or taken as prisoners. The first lines of this epic poem read:

> "Half a league, half a league,
> Half a league onward,
> All in the valley of Death
> Rode the six hundred.
> "Forward, the Light Brigade!
> Charge for the guns!" he said.
> Into the valley of Death
> Rode the six hundred."

You can read the rest of this dramatic poem in its entirety at **www.poetry-foundation.org**.

THE INDIAN MUTINY

Although Queen Victoria's reign is remembered as mostly a peaceful time, England did see violence in other parts of the world besides the few years it spent aiding the Turks during the Crimean War.

Not long after Victoria and Albert's ninth child, Beatrice, was born in 1857, an uprising over the British control in India led to a year of horror and violence. The Indians rebelling in the northern and central provinces were ultimately defeated, and India officially became a British colony.

In the beginning, it seemed England's arrival to India in the past had been good for the economy for both countries. The English came to trade, and control over their business was led by the **East India Trading Company**.

Over time, the British visitors began to think of themselves as residents and became involved in Indian politics, fighting with the French over control and snatching up land and power. Because India wasn't stable or prepared to deal with invaders, by the mid-1700s the English had set up governors over Indian provinces, all under the control of the East India Trading Company.

FAST FACT

In the 19th century, England was a Christian nation, but India was not. At the time of the Indian Mutiny, India was primarily inhabited by those who were Hindu or Muslim. According to historian William Dalrymple, the British Indian Army regiments were made up of up to 85 percent Hindu[28] soldiers. The rebels of the mutiny were later joined by other soldiers and fighters, including Muslims, who wanted religious freedom or war.

At first glance, it seemed like British control in India was good for everyone. They built trading factories and outposts with roads and bridges. Eventually, there were telegraph and railroad lines. At the same time, the British started to claim more and more political power.

Many British officers came to love and respect the Indian people and culture. They learned the languages and respected their beliefs. They under-

28. BBC News, 2006

stood that they were equals and that the British were guests in country that outnumbered them, or at least their own soldiers, five to one.[29]

Officially, the East India Company existed under the permission of the **Mughul Emperor** of India. The company was granted the right to trade and tax. Within the province of Bengal, the English were allowed to function as a government with a governor.

The functioning British government in Bengal made treaties with surrounding rulers and increased its power and land control. By 1848, under the rule of British governor-general, **Lord Dalhousie**, flaring Indian tempers could not be cooled.

FAST FACT

James Andrew Broun-Ramsay, later titled Lord Dalhousie, was an educated aristocratic Scottish politician who served the United Kingdom as President of the Board of Trade in 1845 during the rise of the railroads. By 1846, he was serving in India and became Governor of Bengal and Governor-General over other British generals in other East India Trading Company-controlled provinces (1846-1856). Dalhousie made reforms, or changes, that not only modernized India, but also increased British land holdings and helped India organize itself geographically and politically.

One of Dalhousie's most debated acts was called the **Doctrine of Lapse**. Under this reform, whenever an Indian ruler died without an heir, the British would take over his land holdings. This made the Indians furious, and to add insult to injury, Dalhousie changed laws protecting women and children from cultural-influenced mistreatment, neglect, and even human sacrifice.

---

29. Baird, Julia. 2017

Indians worried more Christian missionaries would come and make things worse. More and more, the people of India began to resent the English because of the changes being made to their way of life.

By 1857, small rebellious acts upon the British increased political tensions. Fires were started around Calcutta in eastern India, and the British believed they were started by rebel arsonists. Then, in February, a difference over religious beliefs struck the match that started the 1857 revolt.

That month, a new British rifle, the **Enfield Musket**, was introduced to the army and forced upon Indian soldiers for use. The rifle used a **cartridge** covered in cow or pork grease. The cartridge held the ammunition for the gun, but it had to be opened by tearing it with the teeth. For the Hindu and Muslim soldiers, this was offensive to their faith.

The Hindu religion considered cows sacred and did not eat beef. Muslims believed it was wrong to eat pork. When over 80 Indian soldiers were sent to prison for refusing to load their rifles with the offensive cartridges, a small army of Indians attacked a group of British officers and marched south to kill more. The mutiny began.

Indian regiments supplied by the British with their own weapons joined the revolt. British men, women, and children in the moving path of the rebels were cruelly murdered, and the emperor, Bahadur Shar, did nothing to stop it. The uprising grew, and the British army was forced to retaliate. Unfortunately, they were just as violent and vengeful, slaughtering both the guilty and the innocent.

Besides shooting or bayoneting Indian rebels, the British used the Indian sentence for mutiny against them. This meant tying prisoners to cannons and setting them off. Other Indians that were not killed on the spot were tortured in cruel acts or games before being executed. Newspapers abroad reported the vicious, inhumane murders of each army against the other, and the world was horrified.

One young officer wrote:

> *"It was literally murder.... I have seen many bloody and awful sights lately but such a one as I witnessed yesterday I pray I never see again. The women were all spared but their screams on seeing their husbands and sons butchered, were most painful.... Heaven knows I feel no pity, but when some old gray bearded man is brought and shot before your very eyes, hard must be that man's heart I think who can look on with indifference...."*[30]

Queen Victoria was sickened by the reports of her own country's actions. Her generals did little to stop the atrocities, and some even approved of it. One general reportedly wrote to his captain: *"All honor to you for catching the king and slaying his sons. I hope you will bag many more!"*[31]

The queen defied the violence of her military leaders. Even though the rebellion was stopped and the emperor ousted, she announced that the cruel torture and sport of Indian rebels was shameful. Although she sent heartfelt sympathy to those British who had lost loved ones, she would not condone cruel revenge doled out by her own people.

A peace treaty was signed in July of 1858. Queen Victoria officially became **sovereign**, or leader, of India, which was now considered a true British colony. The East India Company shut down, and the Crown ruled the people of India with a new Governor-General.

---

30. Newworldencyclopedia.org
31. Newworldencyclopedia.org

To the new governor of India, Lord Canning, Queen Victoria insisted,

"...these should be shown the greatest kindness. They should know there is no hatred to a brown skin, none, but the greatest wish on their queen's part to see them happy, contented, and flourishing."[32]

Lord Canning restored calm and order to the colony. Some leaders felt he went too easy on guilty prisoners because many were freed. Some of the Englishmen and military didn't think of themselves as equal or friendly to the Indians anymore. Instead, they began to believe the British were better, smarter, and more peaceful. The army called Lord Canning "Clemency Canning" because he refused to continue punishing rebel sympathizers after the violence, but the Indians did not feel anyone had gotten away with anything. They called the British revenge on the rebellion, "the devil's wind."

FAST FACT

The Victoria Cross is a medal created by Queen Victoria and Prince Albert in 1856. It is awarded for extreme courage to British military members or people serving under military command. The Victoria Cross was first presented during the Crimean War, but 182 members of British forces and the British Indian Army received it for their bravery during the Indian Mutiny. It is a bronze cross made from a Chinese cannon used by the Russians during the Crimean War, and the queen added a small bronze-shaped "V" above the cross to attach it to its ribbon and pin.

32. Baird, Julia. 2017

CHAPTER SIX

Enemies and Errors

L ike many world leaders, Queen Victoria's own life was in danger on several occasions. Sometimes, the curious or mentally ill would sneak into her gardens or even the palace. Other times, she found herself in true danger of being murdered by obsessed, insane, or angry men, determined to assassinate the Queen of England. Her calm and courageous reaction in every life-threatening situation made the people of the United Kingdom admire and respect her even more.

FAST FACT

The most famous intruder to sneak into Buckingham Palace was a small teenage boy named Edward Jones. He climbed the garden wall and sneaked through open windows into the kitchen or empty halls where he would hide and wait for nighttime. During the night, he prowled through the palace, exploring and stealing. During the day, he hid in cabinets or under furniture. Jones was caught running from the palace with stolen clothes in December of 1838. A year later, he was caught hiding under a sofa by a guard who had been called to search the queen's sitting room after a nurse heard a door creak shut in an empty room. Jones was examined and found to be a troubled but harmless boy. For punishment, he was ordered to perform three months of hard labor, but it didn't stop him. Within a year, he was caught in the palace again; this time hiding in the kitchen after midnight with a handkerchief full of stolen food.

Queen Victoria was attacked eight times by seven different men during her reign. All of them were captured and punished, but none of them were executed. The queen's compassion spared them their lives, and because of her ability to rise above their actions, all seven of them disappeared and were almost forgotten. She became as famous as ever for her nerves of steel and compassionate heart.

EDWARD OXFORD

The first attempt on Victoria's life happened in the summer of 1840, just a few months after she had married Prince Albert. Traveling by carriage to the popular Hyde Park, Victoria was surprised when Albert reached for her in alarm. At first, the young queen thought someone was shooting birds, and she laughed. Then another shot exploded into the back of the carriage wall over her head. Victoria later assured Albert, "I was not the least frightened."[33]

The public was impressed with Victoria's bravery after the shots were fired. She insisted on continuing her trip and returning home on another public road. Later that day, horseback riders in the park saw the royal carriage returning, and they surrounded the queen to escort her safely back to Buckingham Palace.

Immediately after the attack, onlookers in the park captured the young gunman and delivered him to the police. Only 17 years old, the police discovered Edward Oxford belonged to an unofficial political group, or club, called "the New England" or the "Young England." Oxford insisted the club, which believed in an **absolute monarchy**, wanted Victoria dead. He also said that the King of Hanover was a member and plotter, too.

---

33. Baird, Julia. 2017

Edward Oxford's assassination attempt on Queen Victoria is depicted in this painting by G.H. Miles in 1840.

Oxford kept other weapons in his room. He was poor and dreamed of revolution. The newspapers expressed concerns he was a paid assassin from Hanover, Germany, but Oxford later told police he wanted to kill the queen because he didn't believe a woman had the right to rule the United Kingdom.

Edward Oxford was sent to an insane asylum for 27 years. After his release, the government sent him to Australia. It's believed he settled in the city of Melbourne, changed his name, and lived a respectable life as a painter and churchwarden. He later died in 1900 after finding himself in trouble with the law once more after suffering from delusions.

JOHN FRANCIS

The second would-be assassin of Queen Victoria tried to shoot her twice. John Francis was a small, angry-looking young man. The papers reported Francis, the well-known son of the head machinist who operated and repaired machines, at the Theater Royal in Covent Garden, was thought to be respectable. Unknown to police, he had taken a shot at the carriage the day before in Green Park ,but he was caught on his second try on May 30, 1842.

Prince Albert knew a gunman had taken a shot at the queen on May 29, but he could not keep her from continuing her duties. With her security on the lookout, they continued their daily routine the next day. Albert later wrote, "We looked behind every tree, and I cast my eyes round in search of the rascal's face."[34] The precautions did little good.

Francis looked to be decently dressed when arrived at the spot where the royal carriage often passed through London. Onlookers said he began insulting the queen, "by making use of the most horrid language"[35], and that later when the carriage passed by on Constitution Hill, he pulled a pistol from his jacket and fired.

The calm gunman shot at the queen in her carriage from only five steps away, then was promptly tackled by security and the police. He was later determined not to be insane, but angry at his income and status. The court sentenced Francis to be hung, drawn, and quartered. It was a terrible, medieval death, so Queen Victoria insisted on changing his sentence to something she considered more humane.

34. Baird, Julia. 2017
35. Britishmuseum.org

Francis was banished to Australia for life into the criminal settlement of Port Arthur in Tasmania. After 14 years, he was pardoned for his crime and became a somewhat successful carpenter and builder. He died in 1885 of tuberculosis.

JOHN WILLIAM BEAN

Less than two months after being shot at by John Francis, Queen Victoria endured another assassination attempt on Sunday, July 3, 1842, on her way to church. It was not a serious try, and the queen did not come close to being struck by any bullets.

The gunman, John William Bean, escaped the crowd of men who saw him pull a gun out from under a long coat, but he was easy to recognize because he stood only four feet tall with a deformed back. The police searched the homes of young men with handicaps and discovered Bean at his family home in Clerkenwell.

Bean was an educated young man, but he had a hard time finding work. He blamed it on his handicap and decided a half-hearted attempt on the queen's life might bring him the attention he deserved. A reader by nature, Bean had books he'd collected, and he sold them to buy a gun.

Luckily for Victoria, the boy loaded the old gun with a strange mix of tobacco and gunpowder. It didn't fire when he pulled the trigger at the queen's carriage, and he later insisted to police he'd aimed at the ground.

With the many attempts on Queen Victoria's life, the police had to treat a would-be assassin seriously. Bean went to trial and was given 18 months of hard prison labor.

In his later life, Bean lived rather quietly hoping to avoid the attention and memory of his failed attempt to shoot the queen. He stayed in England where he married twice and worked as a **newsvendor**, or newspaper salesman. Bean struggled with depression most of his life, and sadly, he committed suicide by overdosing on **opium** in 1882.

FAST FACT

After Queen Victoria's second escape from an assassin's bullet, the public became concerned with the strange popularity of shooting at the queen. The poet, Elizabeth Barrett Browning, wrote to a friend: "Poor Victoria! ...I hear that people go now to see the poor queen leave the palace for her drive with the disposition to be excited, with an idea of seeing her shot at: there is a crowd at the gates every day![36]

WILLIAM HAMILTON

Several years passed in relative safety for the royal family, but in 1849, another man shot at Queen Victoria as she rode through Hyde Park on the official celebration of her 30th birthday. At half past six in the evening, she was on her way back to Buckingham Palace, and three of her younger children were in the carriage with her.

The crowded streets buzzed with festival goers, or as the papers reported, "holiday folk," when from out of nowhere a man dressed in work clothes, including a flannel jacket and corduroy breeches, shot at the carriage from the same spot as Edward Oxford nine years before. A park keeper managed to overpower the shooter until the police arrested him.

36. Baird, Julia. 2017

The shooter's identity and intentions did not come as a shock. William Hamilton, an Irish immigrant raised in an orphanage, was unhappy with his lack of opportunities, and so he loaded a pistol with gunpowder but no bullets, and shot the weapon to get attention. He told the police he "was tired of being out of work."[37]

Maybe Mr. Hamilton thought he would be sentenced to a secure life in an asylum like previous shooters, but such was not the case. Under a new law, he could be brutally whipped, but once more Queen Victoria had compassion on her perpetrator. Hamilton was shipped to the prison colony of Gibraltar on Spain's west coast where he labored for seven years. Afterward, he was sent to Australia to live out the rest of his days.

FAST FACT

England's criminals were not always sent to prison. The government preferred to hang them or send them away. If one was lucky, he was sent into exile to a foreign country to live in camps called prison colonies.

In 1788, 736 convicts were ordered to be shipped on eleven different ships to the land of Australia with Captain Arthur Phillip. The conditions were so terrible there that the marines and the prisoners almost died of starvation and diseases, but eventually, they learned how to farm, hunt, fish, and survive in the harsh environment.

Captain Phillips went back to England in 1792 believing that he'd created a place where people could live and work together. For the next six decades, about 50,000 people were sent to Australia for punishment. Many found that if they survived the trip, they went on to live quiet, acceptable lives, and the country of Australia developed and grew. Australia became an independent country in 1901.

37. Murphy, Thomas Paul. 2017

ROBERT PATE

Believe it or not, only a year later, poor Victoria was attacked again, and this time she was wounded. On June 27th, 1850, Victoria traveled to Cambridge House to visit a sick uncle. As she left the house with three of her children and a lady-in-waiting, a man broke through the crowd of well wishers and hit her on the head with his cane before she could climb back into the royal carriage.

As it always happened, the crowd instantly seized upon the well-dressed man, even as Victoria stood tall and announced, "I am not hurt!"[38] She would later have a bruise and black eye, but being the monarch she was, she refused to be afraid or change her drives and visits.

The man's name was Robert Pate, and he was a retired army officer who lived nearby in St. James. Pate had suffered a mental breakdown since retiring as a lieutenant from the 10th Hussars, and he was well known for acting peculiar around town and in the city parks. He was examined by doctors who decided he did suffer from mental illness but still understood the difference between right and wrong.

FAST FACT

The trial and mental health of Robert Pate was well-documented. Several witnessed said that Pate was not normal. One of the doctors, Edward Thomas Monro, testified:

> *"I have had five interviews with Mr. Pate since this occurrence—I saw him first on the 2nd of the month at Clerkenwell, and again on the 3rd; and I saw him afterwards in Newgate on the 5th, 8th, and 10th—from my own observation, and from what I have heard to-day, I believe him to be of unsound mind."*[39]

38. Baird, Julia. 2017
39. Starmans, Barbara J. 2017

A month later, Pate, who was no youngster at 30 years old, was found guilty of trying to injure and assault the queen, as well as disturbing the peace. He was sentenced to seven years in the overseas prison of Tasmania, Australia, and so off he went to the far side of the world.

ARTHUR O'CONNOR

The sixth man who tried to harm Queen Victoria was not a man at all, but a 17-year-old Irish boy. Arthur O'Connor was a clerk who lived with his parents in Houndsditch. On February 29, 1872, he jumped over a fence at Buckingham Palace and waited for the 53-year-old queen to return from her drive in the parks.

The inhabitants of the royal carriage and their security suspected nothing as it entered the gates, but O'Connor ran up to the carriage door when it reached the entrance to the palace. He stopped just inches away from the queen and raised his pistol; Victoria bowed her head. Fortunately for the maturing queen, one of her most loyal servants, John Brown, grabbed O'Connor by the neck and threw him to the ground. It was later discovered that the pistol did not work.

FAST FACT

The Earl Granville made an immediate announcement in Parliament that the queen had almost been shot once again:

"The queen showed the greatest courage and composure, and immediately commanded Colonel Hardinge to come down to the Houses of Parliament in order to prevent exaggerated rumours and alarm being spread."[40]

40. The Pall Mall Gazette, 1872

Arthur O'Connor was taken to the police where he claimed he only wanted to scare the queen into releasing Irish prisoners from jail. His parents claimed that he, too, was mentally ill, but it could not be proven in court. This time, the queen's attacker was whipped 20 times with a rod and sent to prison for a year before being transported to Australia.

O'Connor spent years in asylums in New South Wales, Australia, and once wrote the queen a long poem. Mad as a hatter, he wanted her to see what he believed was his worthiness, importance, and brilliance. His letter never made it to her desk.

RODERICK MACLEAN

It was very cold on March 2, 1882, when the last man who would publicly attack Queen Victoria took a shot at her carriage. Victoria arrived at the Windsor train station from London, ready to be greeted by students from Eton College cheering from a festive, carpeted train platform.

As the queen stepped off the train and climbed into her waiting carriage, a shabbily dressed man emerged from the crowd 30 yards away and fired a pistol. A bullet that was never found missed the carriage, and one or two college boys beat the shooter with their umbrellas until he was arrested by Chief Superintendent Hayes of the Windsor Borough Police.

At first, Victoria thought the sound of the gun was an explosion from the train engine. After she was informed of the near miss, she sent a telegram, now a common way to communicate in 1882 London, to Prince Albert.

The March 3, 1882 Belfast News-Letter reported that the queen's telegram to her husband assured him of her safety with no fear or hysterics:

"In case an exaggerated report should reach you, I telegraph to say that, as I drove from the station here a man shot at the carriage, but fortunately hit no one. He was instantly arrested. I am nothing the worse."

The shooter was a small 30-year-old Irishman name Roderick Maclean. Some records list his name as Frederick McLean. He was known to be insane, which meant he had no job or income.

Using what little money he had, he bought a cheap German revolver and loaded it with two bullets, intending to kill the queen.

The court charged Maclean with high treason, but it was clear he was a lunatic. His sentence sent him to Broadmoor Asylum for the rest of his life.

Queen Victoria smiles, amused,
on one of her many carriage rides.

FAST FACT

Queen Victoria was quoted as saying, "It is worth being shot at to see how much one is loved."[41]

CAUSE AND EFFECT

The threats to Queen Victoria's life only made her adoring public love her more. For those who felt unhappy about some of her politics, the attempts on her life helped change their minds about her and respect her. Sometimes the near-death experiences would change public opinion after unpopular actions or decisions from the palace were made.

While the queen's shooters all had fleeting moments of fame up until their trials in the papers, none of them ever went on to become notorious or remembered in the public eye. They all lived long after their sentences because of Victoria's forgiveness, but their stardom was brief and then they became invisible, while her reputation and legacy lived on.

FAST FACT

One of the positive changes that came about because of the attacks on Queen Victoria was new laws. So many of the would-be assassins were mentally ill that more attention was given to those who needed help for their mental health. After the last attempt on her life, Victoria pushed for a clear definition of insanity. Her politics helped define how the legally insane could be prosecuted.

41. Baird, Julia. 2017

ERRORS AND UNPOPULARITY

Queen Victoria inherited the throne of a country that had struggled for centuries over power from within. By the time she took the crown, there were major social issues about equality and freedom. It was a time when the official power of the monarchy diminished, but the influence of royalty over Parliament and the people grew.

The population of the United Kingdom, especially in London, seemed to explode during Victoria's reign. More and more people moved from agriculture to factory work, which meant moving into crowded cities.

Economically, even though changes in business and industrialization slowly improved living conditions, there were still problems with hunger, illness, and crime. Many of the queen's would-be assassins came from those classes who struggled to survive.

Victoria and Albert cared a great deal about the poor, and some of the government programs for them did make life better for a few, but they were far from perfect. **Poorhouses** were provided for the poor and the sick, but often the mentally ill would use them as asylums, too. Entire families sometimes found themselves in the poorhouse, where they had to work to cover their food and living expenses.

These places were almost always over-crowded and filthy. There was little food, and sicknesses spread easily from person to person. Criminals often found refuge in the poorhouse, which endangered the people struggling to survive there, especially young people.

FAST FACT

To be poor in the 19th Century was shameful, and many middle and upper-class people looked down on the less fortunate. It was assumed that poverty came from being sinful or lazy. There was not always enough work during the Victorian Era, even with industrialization, so the uneducated, handicapped, mentally ill, and new immigrants often found themselves in poorhouses with little to no hope.

It wasn't just middle and lower class English families that struggled with hunger: immigrants came for work and found a shortage of food, too. Many came from Ireland, where a terrible disease was ruining potato crops.

The Irish potato famine

The potato was an important food for the United Kingdom. Farmers and others who lived in the rural countryside of Ireland used it as the main sources of their nutrition and income. In 1845, a fungus began to rot the potato harvest, and within a year, over one-third of the harvest was ruined. In other words, one of every three potatoes was inedible.

FAST FACT

Potato blight refers to the fungus that ruins potatoes. It causes spots on the outside of the vegetable, and makes it soggy, black, and rotten on the inside. Today it is called *phytophthora infestans* and is also known to affect tomatoes. Blight is caused by a mix of both warm and humid conditions. This uncommon type of weather in Ireland is always cause for concern for potato farmers.

Many of the potato fields in Ireland were owned by Englishmen who hired landlords and rent collectors to run the properties. When the fungus arrived, the Irish farmers who worked the fields for these lords found themselves unable to feed their families or produce enough crop to pay rent.

The potato blight caused a famine that lasted six years. Millions of people died of hunger and illness, and many more found themselves poor or homeless. As whispers of an Irish rebellion made the palace nervous, the continued ignorance and bias toward the Irish under English rule contributed to more loss of life. Victoria was able to avoid an angry Irish revolution, but approximately one million people left Ireland and immigrated to other countries like America and Canada.

It was unfortunate Queen Victoria was criticized for not doing enough to help Ireland during the potato famine because the government response to the tragedy was handled by Prime Minister Robert Peel and later, Sir John Russell.

FAST FACT

Traders and merchants in the United Kingdom were already frustrated with taxes on corn and other grains before the famine started. The problems in Ireland helped their cause, and soon Prime Minister Peel realized that free trade, especially for food and grains, was important for a country's survival.

Within the first year of the blight, Peel authorized a purchase of £100,000 of corn from America. The shipment arrived late, the grain was difficult to grind, and it took a long time to cook. The poor called it "**Peel's Brimstone.**" In an effort to help the economy, Peel authorized the building of roads, bridges, and canals in Ireland to provide work for the unemployed farmers.

Unfortunately, the workers had a hard time getting paid and still went hungry. There was food available in the form of meat, dairy, and other grains, but no one could afford to buy it. The prime minister also repealed tariffs, or taxes, on corn shipments, but it did little to help the economy.

In 1847, Peel's replacement, Sir John Russell, made quick changes like doing less and letting Ireland recover on its own. He pushed through loan opportunities for the poor and opened soup kitchens. The result was that poor families were unable to pay back the loans and there were uprisings of violence. Russell had to send extra troops into Ireland to stop the violence and found his efforts to be fruitless when the potato blight continued through the end of 1848.

There was a lot of propaganda and blame for the famine in Ireland. One published, angry poem, "The Jacobin's Prayer,"[42] read:

"Avenge the plunder'd poor, Oh Lord!
But not with fire, but not with sword,—
Not as at 'Peterloo' they died,
Beneath the hoofs of coward pride.
Avenge our rags, our chains, our sighs,
The famine in our children's eyes!
But not with sword—no, not with fire!"

Donations came into Ireland from all around the world, but it was too late. By the end of the potato famine in 1851, the Irish population had decreased by over two million people.

---

42. Elliot, Ebenezer. 1833

Crime

Because of poverty and other political problems, violent crime became a major problem in Victorian England, too. There were different classes of criminals. Historians have divided them into murder, burglary, smash and grab, pickpockets, and so on. Even prostitution by desperate women and mothers was considered criminal.

The police found themselves dealing with cold-blooded killers at the time, but new scientific discoveries slowly advanced **forensics**, or investigating techniques. There was poisoning, strangling, and drowning. This was the age of Jack the Ripper and the fictional *Sherlock Homes*.

FAST FACT

Jack the Ripper is the famous nickname for a serial killer in the late 1880s who violently murdered women suspected of prostitution in the poor district of London's Whitechapel district. He was never caught, but his terrible crimes created rumors, stories, legends, and today, even movies and books.

Theft and burglary were serious problems. If people were not safe in their own homes, they were also robbed in coaches, and on boats and trains. Women and children could be kidnapped and forced into prostitution. Even the dead were not safe. Some bodies that disappeared were believed to be the victims of bodysnatching or grave robbing. These corpses were sold to doctors and scientists for study and experiments.

Victorian England had its share of non-violent crime as well. There were pickpockets and beggars. **Mudlarks**, who were often children, scavenged the Thames River that runs through London at low tide to find anything they could sell. They were often forced to search through sewers and any other place a person on the street might drop something valuable.

Con artists swindled money out of fake investors in new areas of commerce like the railroad and trade companies. Grocers or vendors faked the food measurements or quality of the food they sold. Exotic oils and medicines were advertised as miracle cures to people desperate for treatments.

FAST FACT

In 1790, a steam engine factory worker in Cornwall, England, named William Murdock, began experimenting with lighting different kinds of gases to get a safe flame. He found that coal gas worked like magic, and used it to light his house. Eight years later, the factory where he worked, the Soho Foundry, used his gas lighting to light up the inside. A few years later, gas lamps were set up outside to light up around the building.

Almost 20 years after Murdock's great idea, gas lamps lit up the first street in London and over a year later, they were added to the famous Westminster Bridge. Today, over two centuries later, some parts of London are still lit up at night by over 1,500 gas lamps. No one needs to light them one by one like they did in the past, today gas lamps use simple timers.

Because of the growth of crime during Victoria's rule, more manpower was added to the police force, and punishments became more serious and harsh. Called "**Bobbies**" or "Peelers," after Sir Robert Peel who created and grew what would be the modern English police force, they took on more and more responsibilities like lamp lighting, crowd control, and the fire watch.

Partisan politics

Through the years, some of Victoria's politics and meddling in Parliament's business came back to haunt her. People did not grasp that at the time of Victoria's ascension, the role of the Crown in English rule was changing. With her strong personality and independent mind, Victoria didn't hesitate to press her opinion on others whether it was her right or not; when her son, Edward VII, became king, he backed away from trying to manage party politics and began championing causes and representing the people, a trend that continues today for the monarchy.

Sir Robert Peel resigned in 1846 after the failure of the Corn Laws, and the House of Commons in Parliament broke up into different party groups that could not get along or work together. It gave Victoria opportunities to be more involved politically, but she was still limited by what she could and could not do.

During the American Civil War, with the queen's approval, Albert assisted in writing letter to the Union that helped the United Kingdom avoid taking sides in the war. Victoria pressured her own government to stay out of Poland's revolt against its Russian rulers in 1863. A year later, she convinced Parliament to stay out of a war between Prussia and Denmark.

Not everyone liked Victoria and Albert's influence. Later reforms organized the government back into a two-party system. Even then, Victoria met or pressured her leaders to do things she felt were right. That included meeting with the Archbishop of Canterbury to plead for mercy in behalf of religious freedoms, especially in Ireland.

FAST FACT

The Archbishop of Canterbury is the leader of the Church of England.

For a time, one of Victoria's favorite prime ministers, Disraeli, mistakenly convinced her she had more rights than she really did to intervene in the government. She came to believe she could fire her prime ministers and other advisers. She also felt it was her right for her speeches to be her own and not approved by others. Once corrected, the queen stubbornly told her cabinet of ministers that she would "lay down the thorny crown" and quit if they did not see things her way.

Years later, after Albert passed away, Queen Victoria only opened the political season in Parliament seven times, something that she usually did every year. Although the public missed her, many politicians did not.

One leading minister told Victoria's secretary that the people only wanted a queen who looked the part. She was not welcome to take sides in government parties and leaderships. In the final years of her life, Victoria found her passion for politicking once more and became more politically active, just as she had been during Albert's lifetime. She did not cease fighting for what she believed was best for the people of the United Kingdom until the day she died.

CHAPTER SEVEN

Albert Dies Young

Queen Victoria and Prince Albert's happiness would last only a couple of years past their 40th birthdays because of his chronic health problems that took a turn for the worse. The queen continued to focus her energy on raising her big family and depended on her husband for help with the monarchy.

While most of England finally accepted Albert in the years following their marriage, during the Crimean War, the newspapers began to criticize him again. The Great Exhibition had been an enormous success, but doubters expressed concerns that he'd invited so many foreigners to English soil. Albert was still German. He did not ride or dress like the people of his adopted homeland. Sadly, some people even thought his loyalty to Victoria and the children was a weakness.

As Albert grew busier politically, critics of Victoria said she'd lost some of her stubbornness and confidence in state matters. She ignored her critics and trusted her husband to a point where Albert's opinion became more important to Victoria than the advice and counsel of her own ministers. He was so active in the decision-making of the palace and Parliament that he argued and fought with other leaders.

FAST FACT

Queen Victoria thought her husband was so handsome, she was thrilled when the army ordered its soldiers to wear small mustaches like the Prince Consort.

People decided Albert was acting too much like a king, but he made Victoria proud. She loved and adored him to the point of madness. During this time, she recorded in her journal about how serious she took her wedding vows: *"I feel so impressed by the promise I have made to love, cherish, honour, serve and obey my husband.*[43]

Albert and Victoria both turned 40 years old in 1859. They spent alone time enjoying visits to Balmoral. There in the Scottish Highlands, they sneaked into inns disguised as regular travelers, and when they were at the castle, they socialized with their neighbors and enjoyed bits and pieces of normal life. They danced for Victoria; they walked and hiked for Albert.

Life was far from perfect, though, especially for the Prince Consort. His life-long illnesses with stomach pains and fevers began to catch up with him. He worked so hard that the stress gave him headaches and sometimes even made him vomit. It was hard for Victoria to understand his health problems. They were not only opposite in personality, but different in stamina. Where Albert was ill most of the time, Victoria glowed with energy and health. It was his mental and emotional strength that she depended on when her emotions were weak.

---

43. Baird, Julia. 2017.

Victoria and Albert pose for a photograph
near the end of the Prince Consort's life.

The next year, in 1860, Albert went to visit his brother in Coburg. He was tired and told his family he felt like it would probably be the last time he would see Germany. They were alarmed at how thin and frail he'd become. During the trip, Albert was in a carriage accident and had such a hard time recovering that everyone suddenly realized he might be sick enough to die.

The constant sickness made the Prince Consort want to die. He told Victoria that "I do not cling to life"[44] any longer. He didn't care about death, but he worried about his family so much he couldn't sleep. The sick prince didn't stop working though, and that made him grumpy and short-tempered.

---

44. Baird, Julia. 2017

The queen became discouraged. She tried to comfort him and avoided upsetting him in any way, but the mysterious disease took over by the late fall of 1861. Albert kept to his rooms most of the time with pain in his stomach, back, and sometimes his legs.

On November 30th, Albert wrote the last political letter of his career that many feel is the most important thing he ever did. The United States was in a civil war, and Queen Victoria had ordered her kingdom not to take sides. Things became serious for England when a northern United States warship captured a British warship and took two prisoners.

Victoria and Albert did not want war and neither did the American president, Abraham Lincoln. Albert wrote a gracious, forgiving letter telling Lincoln that England would assume that it was a minor mistake and no harm had been intended. It saved his queen from another war.

A day or so later, Albert became so sick only strong drugs would relieve his pain, fever, and constant chills. Four days later, he was so lifeless he would not communicate with his doctors or family.

The palace doctors did not tell Victoria the full truth. It was suspected Albert suffered from some type of bowel fever, but they told the queen they expected him to make a big improvement soon.

Albert didn't get any better. He had to rest against Victoria's shoulder to take a drink. He gasped for air and spoke little. On December 13th, 1861, Albert was so weak he could hardly take a breath. The queen called their oldest son, Bertie, to come at once. Within two hours, he and the Princesses Alice and Helena were there, too.

Gathered around Albert's bedside, Victoria leaned up against him. When he did not wake after she kissed his forehead, she began to cry. Minutes later, the prince took his last breath and passed away before the clock struck 11 that night.

Queen Victoria collapsed in grief. Eventually, she was carried from his room to be put to bed, but not before crying, "There is no one to call me Victoria now."[45] She later ran to the room of their youngest daughter and clutched the four-year-old in her arms.

FAST FACT

The cause of death written on Prince Albert's death certificate was "typhoid fever." Typhoid fever is caused by bacteria that lives in and spoils,\ food and water. No one else at the palace became sick with the disease after Albert. Today, modern medical theories suggest that Prince Albert died from Crohn's Disease (digestive inflammation) or stomach cancer.

That night, the bells of St. Paul's Cathedral tolled the sad news. People didn't realize the prince was so close to death. Now Christmas would be dark and heartbreaking. What they could not predict, however, was that their strong-willed queen would fall into a darkness so deep she would barely find her way back out again.

45. Baird, Juilia. 2017

Prince Albert is photographed here one year before his death.

THE ROYAL RECLUSE

Prince Albert of Saxe-Coburg and Gotha, the love of Queen Victoria's life, was buried on December 23rd, 1861. As much as she worshiped him, Victoria could not bring herself to attend the funeral.

A simple honor guard transferred his remains in a hearse pulled by six horses from a vault at Windsor Castle's chapel to a **mausoleum** at Frogmore, a royal retreat with gardens within the boundaries of Windsor's park.

Four royal carriages followed Albert to his final resting place. The somber party was escorted by the **2nd Regiment of Life Guards** and the **1st Battalion of Scots Fusiliers**. Those who had the heart to attend the funeral included some of his children, government ministers, and foreign ambassadors.

One foreign newspaper reported,

> *"A prince like this, a man like this, did not stand in need of a torchlight funeral, or of those mediæval pageantries so loved and courted by other monarchs; he knew that he had left behind him an example of domestic virtue and the fulfilment of duty, the memory of which will live in the hearts of all, which could not be increased by anything that the pomp of funerals could bestow. All was simple as became his calm and philosophic mind..."*[46]

All of England seemed to be blanketed in black. Shows were canceled, and flags flew at half-mast. The newspapers wrote stories about Albert's gifts, hard work, and determination. The people and the press now realized he'd never been given the credit or respect that he deserved.

Prince Albert had promoted the middle class and eased the power of the aristocrats. He'd wisely advised the queen to be careful and thoughtful in her involvements with other countries. Along with Victoria, Albert had used his wisdom and influence to network with other European leaders and promote friendship and peace.

During Albert's reign as Prince Consort, he'd improved life for the country's poor and the education system. The arts and sciences had never been in better hands. Now, the monarchy's reputation for moral values and a family-centered life was a bitter star in England's sky of grief.

---

46. The New Zealand Spectator and Cook's Strait Guardian, 1862.

FAST FACT

Prince Albert is popular for introducing the Christmas tree to England, although the wife of George III had brought over the practice from Germany as early as 1800. Albert brought attention to the tradition again in 1840 when he shipped in fir trees from Coburg and decorated them. The fancy tree decorations, including burning candles, were reported in descriptive detail in the newspapers every year after that. By the 1850s, almost everyone set up Christmas trees in their homes.

No one grieved harder or longer for Prince Albert than Victoria. Though it was common for women to mourn deeper for their loved ones in this era, the 42-year-old queen showed her pain in obsessive ways, both in private and in public.

Sadly, the room where Albert died never changed again while Victoria lived. To respect his memory, she ordered hot water, fresh towels, and flowers for him every morning and his clothes were laid out every day. The last entry in one of his personal books was left open on that page on a table. A glass he drank out of before he died stayed by the bed. She also put his photo by his bed. Victoria never wore any other color besides black for the rest of her life. Even her stationary was printed with black borders. She never attended another ball.

To keep him immortal, the queen ordered busts and statues of her husband to be displayed everywhere, although he was never a king. As was commonly done for those of royal birth or other fame, she had a **cast**, or model, taken of his face and hands. The **Royal Albert Hall, a concert venue,** and the **Albert Memorial,** which featured a 14-foot statue of the prince, were built in his memory. Army regiments took on his name, and even cities and lakes around the globe, like **Lake Albert** in Africa, were named after him. Victoria kept his star burning while she became a shadow.

Above is a photo of the interior of Royal Albert Hall, a famous concert venue in England named for the late Prince Consort.

Special honors awarded to Prince Albert include:

- The Knight of the Garter; an award for successful service to the United Kingdom

- The Knight of the Thistle; an Scottish equivalent of the Order of the Garter

- The Knight of Saint Patrick; an Irish order for chivalry and service

- The Great Master of the Order of the Bath; a British order of chivalry and service

- The Knight Companion of the Star of India; an order of chivalry created by Queen Victoria

- The Knight Grand Cross of the Order of Saint Michael and Saint George;an award for those holding high positions of command or office for non-military service

AVOIDING THE SPOTLIGHT

The once vibrant and social butterfly queen now kept to herself. She said everyone stared and pitied her every time she set a foot out the door. She was overwhelmed with royal duties without Albert's help and suffered from headaches and sleeplessness. Everything that he'd touched or loved distressed her to the point of making her ill. Some things had to be put away so she could bear his loss.

FAST FACT

"Break not, for thou art Royal but endure…"[47] The poet, Alfred Tennyson was a good friend of Albert and Victoria. He dedicated one of his poetry books to Albert, calling him "Albert the Good." His views on death comforted Queen Victoria, but his lines for her in Albert's dedication gave her the most courage.

After the funeral, when the country's ministers cautiously came calling, Victoria informed them she could not meet for another six months. She threatened them with sickness and death if they changed prime ministers while she mourned. Government activity slowed to a halt, and the queen did not appear again publicly for two years. England began to murmur.

The *Times* newspaper expressed the frustration of the people and politicians:

" The living have their claims, as well as the dead. It is impossible for a recluse to occupy the British throne, without a gradual weakening of that authority which the sovereign has been accustomed to expect."[48]

---

47. Dyson, Hope. 2014
48. Baird, Julia. 2017

For several years, Victoria struggled through day-to-day duties and avoided the spotlight. A royal gloom settled over the English throne. By 1864, Victoria had earned the nickname, "The Widow of Windsor." Even though she'd opened Parliament decade after decade, she refused to make an appearance. Her robust health had been robbed by Albert's early death, and she struggled to find the spirit of her youth to help her carry on.

The people around Victoria knew she was stronger than she gave herself credit for. Today, historians feel that the queen struggled with nerves and conditions like **social anxiety** that weren't understood at the time. It's believed that her physical health was less affected than even she knew. It was her emotions that ruled her life.

Over time, and with the love and support of her family, friends, and even a prime minister, Victoria began to wake up from her long, sad sleep. She visited Albert's grave every day, surrounded herself with her children, and eventually, she found a level of peace where she felt she could begin to function.

People, especially politicians, began to whisper that Victoria would never be able to rule again without Albert's help. Some critics began to push her to give up the crown. It had the opposite effect. The old stubbornness in "Little Drina" again reared its head. She decided to work. The recovering widow wrote, "Yes, while life lingers in this shattered frame, my duties shall be done fearlessly."[49]

Victoria finally seemed to turn a corner on her long mourning when her eldest son, Bertie, the future king and Prince of Wales, became sick and

49. Baird, Julia. 2017

nearly died. It happened 10 years to the month after his father died. Bertie's recovery amazed everyone; his mother attended a thanksgiving service in public afterward for the first time since Albert's death. Around the same time, one of the assassination attempts on Victoria's life occurred not long after. It shifted public opinion back into a positive, hopeful light.

When all was said and done, it was Prince Albert who had been everything to Victoria during the happiest years of her life. More than a husband, he'd acted as her partner, best friend, secretary, advisor, and foreign minister. She'd turned to him for advice for the kingdom, as a woman, a wife, and a mother. Despite her iron will and independence, she always listened and acted on his wisdom and counsel. For the rest of Queen Victoria's life, there would be only three men who would be able to understand her grief and reach through it to win her heart and loyalty.

Albert and Victoria face each other in
Buckingham Palace in 1854.

SPECIAL FRIENDS

John Brown, the Scottish ghillie

In 1848, when Victoria and Albert set their sights on buying Balmoral, a man who worked for the estate became a part of their royal household because he hunted and fished with Prince Albert. His name was John Brown, and he was devoted to both the Prince Consort and Queen Victoria.

After Albert died, the bond John Brown had with the royal family became obvious as he helped the queen overcome her grief while she mourned at Balmoral. Despite the fact he was far from royal and not even English, he would become Victoria's most trusted companion and best friend for the next 20 years of her life.

John Brown was a Scottish **ghillie**. A ghillie is an outdoorsman who accompanies hunters or fishermen on trips, much like a guide or assistant. Letters and paintings remember him as a tall, muscular man with short, curly hair. He wore a beard and a kilt. After a riding accident in the Scottish Highlands, Victoria spent time recovering at Balmoral Castle where she grew closer to Brown, who became her official servant.

Victoria struggled with being social and brave for a long time after Albert's death, but with time, and Brown's help, the worst of her grief became bearable. Although she wouldn't attend formal balls, she began to dance again. The ghillie took her riding, climbing, and boating, and eventually would walk, dine, and dance with her.

Not everyone approved of Victoria and Brown's strange friendship. Her own children thought he was too common and rough, especially with his strong Scottish accent. They accused him of being disrespectful to Victoria because he spoke to her like she was anybody else instead of a royal. They believed John Brown drank too much alcohol and fussed too much.

John Brown poses for a photo in his traditional Scottish kilt.

The queen didn't care what anyone thought. In public, Brown acted as her bodyguard. He was the footman who saved her life when Arthur O'Conner approached her carriage and fired at her in 1872. He was also alongside her at the train station in 1882 when Roderick Maclean took a shot at her and missed.

In private, the couple walked, talked, and even argued. They drank together, too. Now Victoria had someone she could talk to and trust with her secrets. The queen and the servant spent private time together and became almost inseparable.

FAST FACT

In 1882, Queen Victoria created the Victoria Devoted Service Medal and presented it to John Brown for saving her life, which he did more than once. The award was never given to anyone else.

Although he was seven years younger, John Brown was not destined to outlive Queen Victoria. During the winter of 1883, the queen sent him out into the freezing weather to find men who'd attacked **Lady Florence Dixie**, a popular but controversial aristocrat who, at the time, lived less than three miles from Windsor Castle. Afterward, Brown came down with a terrible cold that developed into a more serious illness called **erysipelas** that swelled up his face and ears. He died a few days later at 56 years old.

Queen Victoria was shattered over Brown's unexpected death. At the time, she'd been recovering from a fall down some stairs that had left her almost unable to walk. She could hardly stand up, and she had no trusted servant to carry her.

Victoria insisted that John Brown was the truest friend she'd ever had in her life. He'd devoted his life to seeing that she was comfortable and had everything she wanted and needed. Now she felt truly alone with no husband and no best friend.

The queen would always remember Brown as more than a servant. She wanted the public to remember his service, too. Victoria decided to write a book about Brown's life to honor him, but her advisors protested that it wouldn't be proper. This time she listened, but she had his image recreated in statues, paintings, and pins.

FAST FACT

Today, visitors can view a bronze, life-sized statue of John Brown at the Balmoral estate in Scotland.

In his lifetime, John Brown was awarded medals, a doubled salary, and his own home at Balmoral for his service and dedication to Queen Victoria. He would never take the place of her Albert, but his friendship was a special treasure that brought Victoria back from the edge of a dark, gloomy despair and made her want to live again.

The Empress of India

The Empress of India was a not a friend of Victoria's. In 1874, the phrase became her new title. The queen felt honored and thrilled. She'd wanted such a name since the United Kingdom had taken control of India after the Indian Wars, but the liberals in parliament had fought against the idea.

The official title came about through one of the queen's most trusted advisors who she'd worked with closely since Albert's death: Benjamin Disraeli. Disraeli had become prime minister again when his party, the conservatives, won in 1874, and he took the spot of scowling William Gladstone who'd irritated Victoria for years. This amused Victoria. She and Disraeli had gotten on well before, and they became even closer now.

Working once again with Disraeli, Victoria became just as strong a Tory as she'd been a Whig when she was a young girl. She'd become more conservative through the years and cared deeply about the working class. Disraeli's business friendship filled a hole in her royal duties and decisions that Albert had left behind. The two worked together as a formidable team.

Much was accomplished during Disraeli's 1874 10-year term as PM. Most importantly, England avoided a war with Russia when it invaded Turkey again.

In May of 1876, thanks to Disraeli, Queen Victoria was officially awarded the Empress title through Parliament. The act was announced and publicized by Disraeli, who'd fought to get it approved.

FAST FACT

Queen Victoria really wanted the title, "Empress of Great Britain, Ireland, and India," but Prime Minister Disraeli convinced her it would be a bad idea. He believed the Indian nation needed to feel like they had their own ruler and not just attached to some distant land or monarchy.

Some people felt the title was silly. Others complained that she only wanted to elevate herself above her Russian daughter-in-law, the Grand Duchess Marie, who was titled "Her Imperial Highness." It was also understood that Victoria's own daughter, Victoria, would also become an empress when her husband inherited the Prussian throne.

As was her way, Queen Victoria ignored the criticism of politics and papers because she felt the title was well-deserved. She signed her orders "VRI" which stood for *Victoria, Regina et Imperatrix.*

Not long afterward, Disraeli was replaced once more by William Gladstone, but it didn't matter. The queen had worked through her grief and dislike of political activities. Queen Victoria had fully awakened and by 1880, she was fully invested in the details of ruling the government and her country on her own.

Karim 1887

Within five years of losing John Brown, Victoria again became close with another servant, who also became a trusted friend. **Hafiz Mohammad Abdul Karim** came to England to serve dinners to important heads of state and educate the queen on the exciting aspects of life in India. Victoria was obsessed with the exotic domain she'd ruled for about a decade, and she wanted to learn more about Indian culture and ways of life because she would never be able to travel there. It was too far and dangerous for a queen.

Born in 1909, in Agra, India, Abdul Karim was the son of a humble hospital assistant. He worked as a jail clerk in Agra, but he dreamed of much more. When his supervisor had the opportunity to travel to England and meet the queen, Karim jumped at the chance to be one of two representatives to serve on the royal staff.

Karim was presented to Victoria with another Indian servant as a "gift," but the maturing, curious woman soon decided the tall, serious young man could offer much more assistance to her than just serving dishes and drinks. She asked him serious questions, and he provided as much detail as he could, which delighted her sharp intellect.

Karim was proud of his heritage and not only taught Victoria about what life was like in India, but he also cooked exotic curry dishes and taught her his native language, **Hindustani**. Soon, Victoria felt as fond of Karim as she did any of her children, and she promoted him to serve as her personal clerk with a raise in his salary. He was officially titled "Munshi and Indian Clerk to the Queen Empress." Always at her side, he even served her meals.

FAST FACT

There are 22 official languages in India, including Assamese, Bengali, Bodo, Dogri, Gujarati, Hindi, Kannada, Kashmiri, Konkani, Maithili, Malayalam, Meitei (Manipuri), Marathi, Nepali, Odia, Punjabi, Sanskrit, Santali, Sindhi, Tamil, Telugu, and Urdu. However, it is estimated there are over 800 languages and dialects still in use.

The royal household, including family and other servants, despised Karim. He had no previous experience, no record of service, and no recommendations. They hadn't liked John Brown because he was a commoner, but to answer to a brown-skinned man and even sit at the same table with him at dinners sparked outrage and prejudices.

Queen Victoria sits with Abdul Karim standing near her in July 1893, less than a decade before her death.

Karim didn't let others' opinions get in his way. He eventually became one of Victoria's secretaries. While he did serve Victoria with total dedication, he also demanded that he and his family members be compensated. This meant he expected to have royal privileges.

Karim attended meetings, parties, and other royal functions. He could carry a sword and wear medals. If he was seated with guests he considered lower than himself, he would leave and later complain to Queen Victoria. Anxious to satisfy him, Victoria ordered that the clerk was provided housing for himself and his wife on several of the royal properties. Some of the rooms granted to him were John Brown's old rooms. The Indian servant was even known to travel in a royal coach and with a footman, which infuriated others in Victoria's circle.

On one occasion, Karim requested thousands of doses of opiates, like morphine, be shipped to his father in India. Although Victoria's advisors — and personal doctor — declared the request to be unusual and suspicious, Karim got his wish. Victoria later made sure his father received a **pension**. She even looked the other way when he asked that his aunts be allowed to come live with him in England. They weren't really his aunts; they were other wives.

Despite protests from other royals and advisors, Queen Victoria, now in her 80s, kept Karim close by. The dedicated man entertained her, made her laugh, listened to her advice, and shared his exotic lifestyle and family with her. There was no doubt that the Munshi made the queen happy.

FAST FACT

Queen Victoria loved Indian curries and other cuisines. She studied the Indian language of Urdu for 13 years, but because of this, many Indians remember it is a language of slavery.

Letters to Karim from Victoria were signed "Your loving mother" as well as other phrases of friendship. She encouraged stories about him to be printed in the papers and had pictures and paintings of him done. She even involved him in matters of India politics and allowed him access to important papers and information. This particularly concerned the queen's oldest son, Bertie, as well as the prime minister.

Tempers in the royal household reached the boiling point about 10 years after Karim's arrival. As Queen Victoria planned a trip to Europe, the rest of the palace rebelled at the idea of the Munshi attending the queen on the journey. Victoria's children, advisors, and even personal doctor refused to go or even eat with the servant anymore.

Victoria became stressed. Finally, her doctor, Dr. James Reid, who had tended to her for years and would take care of her affairs at her death, sat down with Victoria and informed her of some of the details of Karim's life and how he carried out his duties.

Karim had told everyone that his father was a surgeon in the British Army. It was only now the truth his father was just a helper came to light. Besides that, the Munshi had overspent his allowance, not provided receipts for his spending, and was blamed for leaking sensitive political information to some of his contacts. Dr. Reid also pointed out that when one of Karim's relatives had stolen a brooch that belonged to Victoria, she'd blamed it on a simple Indian custom that accepted taking things that were left lying around.

Queen Victoria tried to understand. She wasn't pleased with some of Karim's choices, but she still considered him a trusted friend. Victoria spent almost two years trying to prove Karim was not guilty of any of their accusations, but it was all in vain. The royal household held the Munshi at arms-length, so Victoria was forced to be more careful in her decisions.

Karim served Queen Victoria for 15 years until she passed away. In her last instructions, she requested he walk in her funeral procession, but Bertie saw to it that her most of her wishes were not kept. Although the Munshi was allowed to see Victoria put to rest in her coffin, Karim and his family were sent back to India right after she died. The Munshi lived out the rest of his days on land that'd been granted to him by the Empress of India. He died at a young 46 years old.

Whether it was jealousy, prejudice, or the fact he was common, the family of Queen Victoria ordered her letters to and from Karim burned. His name was removed from her journals. They also got rid of paintings and any other references of the friends' history. It would be almost 100 years before anyone remembered the mother-and-son bond of the English monarch and a young Indian man.

Abdul Karim faithfully kept his own records in India. In 1897, he wrote in his journal:

"I've been but a sojourner in a strange land and among a strange people... While I record my life, I cannot but call to mind the many honours which have fallen to my lot and all through the great goodness of Her Majesty."[50]

---

50. Miller, Julie. 2017

CHAPTER EIGHT

Queen Victoria

The British Empire expanded from the Caribbean islands to Australia and Africa during Queen Victoria's reign. At the peak of the United Kingdom's reach and power, Victoria ruled one-fourth of the populated world. This meant she stood as a figurehead over 400 million people.

Despite Albert's influence and decision-making during her reign as a married woman, Victoria accomplished a great deal on her own, becoming her most politically active (and stubborn) after recovering from the years mourning Albert's death. Some of her achievements created changes that improved the quality of life that the people of England enjoy today. Wages went up, housing became more affordable, and welfare improved.

As women followed Victoria's lead on standing up for herself, they pushed forward the women's **suffrage** movement, which the queen publicly would not endorse. However, the queen, who would not remove the vow to obey her husband from her wedding ceremony, did encourage and fight for changes in the laws that affected the lives of women.

For example, during Victoria's rule, it became a legal right for women to claim power over the safety and protection of their own bodies. Where once a husband could claim control, even sell a wife in centuries past, women won the right to be individuals and considered separate from their spouses.

FAST FACT

As women saw their right to be recognized as equals improve during the 19th century, they also saw more fairness in cases of divorce or abandonment. Historically, fathers were awarded custody of the children in all situations of broken marriages, no matter who was at fault. The *Infant Custody Act of 1839* recognized that children should not always be given to the father in the event of divorce. Women were granted the right to fight for the custody of their children up to the age of seven years old and were awarded the right to at least see their children if they were older. While it was not completely fair, it was a step in the right direction.

Another step toward progress for women occurred in Parliament in 1870 and 1882 with the **Married Women's Property Acts**. The 1870 law allowed married women to have power over any money that they earned instead of being required to turn it over to their husbands.

In 1882, this law was expanded to include property. It made a historical change on how women inherited property and what they could do with it. With this new act, women could inherit property from their families and not have to turn it over to their husbands upon tying the knot. In another massive change, 12 years later in 1894, women who owned property were given the right to vote — a privilege only landed gentry, or men with property, enjoyed.

LABOR LAWS

The Industrial Revolution pulled back the curtain on the terrible effects of overworked employees. Forced to work long hours — as many as 12 hours in a day — the old laws applied to men, women, and even small children. During Victorian rule, changes were made in Parliament that lowered the workday from 12 hours to eight. Victoria worked to improve safety and fair treatment. These changes sparked recognition of discrimination and bias that would be addressed in the decades to come. Most importantly, Victorian changes focused on protecting small children from being used in slave-like conditions.

FAST FACT

Victorian children worked and often died in coal mines, factories, mills, even while sweeping chimneys. They also learned trades by working long hours for seamstresses, farmers, potters, and shoe and hat makers. Little ones worked as house servants or toiled on the railroads and in the shipyards. Sometimes they were kidnapped or forced to work for criminals.

It was considered normal for children to work long days beside adults during the 18th and 19th centuries. At that time, children without any inheritances or means to higher education were expected to have a job. As rights for young children increased, so did opportunities for education, at long last.

FAST FACT

In 1881, a businessman named Thomas Agnew organized the Liverpool Society for the Prevention of Cruelty to Children. It was popular and effective; it became a national society in 1891 with the full support of Queen Victoria and country.

CRIME AND PUNISHMENT

Just as Queen Victoria showed compassion for the men who made assassination attempts on her life, she fought for changes in crime and punishment in the courtrooms. While death had been the common sentence for many crimes in centuries past, during Victoria's reign, at least 200 crimes with the sentence of the death were changed or removed from the law. No longer would a child be hung for theft or a hungry man sent to his death for **poaching**.

The British did believe in punishment, but as positive steps were made toward equality and for human rights, torture and death became seen as medieval and cruel. More jails, called **gaols**, were built. Transportation to a faraway prison camp, often in an underdeveloped colony, took the place of hanging for most serious crimes outside of murder.

Lesser crimes that once called for hanging now had penalties such as hard labor, physical punishment, or military duty. A sentence to labor might mean working in the dockyards or along the Thames River — if one was lucky enough not to be sent to Australia.

FAST FACT

Between 1735 and 1964, records of England and Wales list 10,935 men and women as being sentenced to hang for their crimes.[51]

---

51. Capitalpunishment.org. 2017

A sentence for physical punishment usually meant a private whipping, as times had changed and public floggings or being locked down in the **stocks** was considered cruel and old-fashioned. Another alternative for justice was to force a criminal to serve in the army or navy. The navy was in such short supply of sailors that it needed to man ships and fight that a criminal could often receive a pardon for joining the service and serving at sea.

FAST FACT

The Abolition of Death Penalty Act ended the death penalty in England on December 16, 1969.[52]

FAILURES

Despite her best attempts to be a fair and compassionate ruler, Victoria made mistakes. Unfortunately, many of them cost millions of people their livelihoods, great pain, or their lives. It is interesting to note that most of her failures occurred after Albert's death and fall under international relations, war, or the stretching arm of the British Empire as it gobbled up territory after territory.

Tragically, there were mass deaths of **indigenous** peoples in the colonies and countries of England around the world during Victoria's reign. These included the natives of Australia and islands of the Pacific, Native Americans in Canada, and South American tribes in Uruguay, Paraguay, and Argentina. Also included in the massive death count are indigenous members from China and African countries.

---

52. Capitalpunishment.org. 2017

FAST FACT

Between 1870 and 1914 the United Kingdom grew from controlling a mere 10 percent of Africa to an astonishing 90 percent.[53]

The people of Africa were afflicted with the most horrific war crimes of the era. The continent was rich in ivory, gold, and diamonds and had exotic animals, food, and spices. At the end of the 19th century, England fought to control its territory from African rebels as Germany and France tried to hold on to their own African land, too. Millions of Africans died during the fight to control their respective countries.

Supporters of Victorian history point the finger of blame for the torture and murder of so many African people on Queen Victoria's cousin, King Leopold II. He was the oldest son of Victoria's beloved Uncle Leopold and the ruler of Belgium. Cousin Leopold was not even well liked at home; he was accused of being greedy, demanding, self-serving, and proud. Most of the English court found him disgusting.

In Africa, cousin Leopold forced people into slavery to produce ivory and rubber in the Congo. He taxed his workforce heavily. Punishment for failure to work or meet production numbers meant the removal of body parts or death. Victoria did little to publicly shame or stop his tyrannical rule. It is estimated that about 10 million Africans died under his authority.[54]

53. Baird, Julia. 2017.
54. Baird, Julia. 2017.

FAST FACT

Rather than grieve, people cheered in the streets during the funeral procession of King Leopold II.

It is a stain on Queen Victoria's legacy that so many millions of human beings in other countries under the rule of the United Kingdom lost their lives to the expansion and wealth of an empire.

MODERN ADVANCEMENTS AND ACHIEVEMENTS

Besides the Great Exposition, Queen Victoria's reign embraced the times and encouraged study and invention. In her lifetime, she saw women enter the fields of science, law, and medicine. There were more inventions and discoveries for her to examine and enjoy than any other king or queen that came before her.

FAST FACT

An Englishman named George Stephenson built a train engine in 1814, which he tinkered with until he could operate it at 35 miles per hour. The first passenger railroad in England opened in 1829, shrinking the 60-hour trip across England for coaches to only 10 hours. No wonder Albert and Victoria purchased their own train cars!

Transportation options and other travel conveniences exploded during Victoria's reign. Where once man got from place to place on horseback or other beasts of burden like donkeys, camels, or elephants, there were now railroads with puffing engines and ships powered by steam instead of wind. A German invented an automobile prototype in 1885. In 1896, Henry

Ford would build his first automobile in the United States of America. Sadly, Queen Victoria would die just a few years before the Wright brothers would fly their airplane on the banks of South Carolina.

FAST FACT

Steam powered ships began crossing the Atlantic Ocean between America and the United Kingdom in 1838. The infamous ship, *Titanic*, would sink 11 years after Queen Victoria's death.

Electricity, specifically electric lighting, became popular later in Victoria's reign, although she did not care to use it. She also saw and used the quick telegraph and later delighted in the invention of the telephone. In fact, the inventor, **Alexander Graham Bell**, was invited to Osborne House to show and test his telephone for the queen in 1878. For the experiment, songs were played on a piano and sung from the nearby cottage for Queen Victoria to hear from the house.

FAST FACT

Thomas Edison patented the first record player, the phonograph, the same year he patented the telephone in 1878. Called a gramophone in England, it was improved by Alexander Graham Bell and used to play disc-shaped records of music. It is believed that Queen Victoria made a recording for the gramophone around 1888, although those who have heard it understood very little, besides "Greetings Britons..."[55]

Machinery and other household devices came into existence during the Victorian age that would change how we live today. Near the end of her

---

55. Dash, Mike. 2011.

life, the queen saw how the typewriter, camera, and even the electric sewing machine changed how people lived and worked.

LITERACY AND WEALTH

During Queen Victoria's reign, the ability to read and write became important to the lower classes. Once a skill only available to the upper classes or the highly educated, Victoria's fight for equality meant education was more available to working children and young adults.

As the Industrial Revolution caught on, so did letter writing and clerking. The mail, or "Penny Post," allowed letters to be sent from place to place for only a penny. Paper and ink became more affordable. Most importantly, the working class had opportunities to move up in management, and this required reading and writing.

At the same time, the publishing industry began to boom. Newspapers, magazines, and books could be manufactured cheaply and used for education and entertainment. The written word began to narrow the gap between the upper classes and those below them.

FAST FACT

Because books could be expensive, lending libraries became popular in the 18th century for those who read but did not have the extra money to collect books. Later, as printing costs went down during the Industrial Revolution, elegant bookstores, like *The Temple of Muses* in London, were all the rage in Victorian England. Visitors could browse through shelves full of books for sale to the affluent reader who had too much money to visit a simple borrowers' library.

There were some in aristocratic circles who did not believe everyone had the right to learn to read and write. They worried that the lower class would consider themselves on equal footing with the nobility, an idea that the unprejudiced queen would certainly not agree with.

On the other hand, there were some lower-class families that felt education was a waste and would only lead to crime or hopeless daydreams. The success of industrialization and Queen Victoria's stand on education slowly changed their ideas. Reading and writing became a necessary and available skill for those who wanted more than to work on the factory lines, and over time, those people sought out those who could teach them to read and write.

FAST FACT

In the year 1650, literacy rates, or the ability to read and write, were esti-mated to be about 53 percent in Great Britain. That's just about half of the population. Amazingly, at the time of Queen Victoria's birth in 1819 over 150 years later, the percentage was still the same. By the time of the queen's death in 1901, literacy in England had jumped to over 80 percent![56]

Reading, writing, and publishing changed the literacy rate and improved the quality of living during Queen Victoria's reign. It would affect the prosperity of England and the lives of generations to come.

Wealth

Queen Victoria and Prince Albert fought energetically for class equality under the guise of education and literacy during the Victorian reign. Because of the Industrial Revolution and their beliefs, a new middle class grew up and prospered, creating wealthy, respected families who had no royal blood at all.

---

56. Roser, Max. 2014.

FAST FACT

No longer defined as rich or poor, four social classes developed during the Victorian age: noble aristocrats with royal bloodlines, a wealthy middle class (usually from trade, government positions, or inheritances), a working middle class, and the lower class who lived in poverty.

Queen Victoria's rule brought a new era to the United Kingdom where it was possible for a commoner to have a successful, influential career or life. England found itself a rich and successful empire both at home and abroad. A focus on the arts, leisure, and politics, while servants ran the household, became the norm for many families even in the middle class.

The wealthiest of Victorian England owned land and large homes. They owned jewels, wore expensive clothing, ate well, and traveled. The middle class, like the upper class, had fine things. Men worked and socialized together while women focused on raising respectable children, running the staff that maintained their homes, and admiring their husbands. Throughout the upper classes there were parties, networking, and matchmaking.

FAST FACT

During the Victorian age, there was a wide gap in wages between different jobs in middle classes. Around 1880, a worker at factory might make just $8 per month, where a professional in business or law could make as much as $166.[57]According to inflation estimates, $166 equals about $3,802.91 at today's rate.

---

57. Victorianera.org

One drawback for the middle class was that wealth could be lost just as easily as it was earned. It wasn't a far fall from one class down into the other. A failed business or bad investment could ruin a family. A widowed middle class woman who had once enjoyed many of life's luxuries could find herself taking in sewing or other types of domestic work in order to survive.

Fortunately, with changes during Victoria's reign, those in poverty now had a more of a chance to succeed through hard work, education, and good old-fashioned luck.

CHAPTER NINE

A Jubilee is One Great Party

In 1887, Queen Victoria celebrated her first jubilee. It was the queen's 50ᵗʰ **Golden Jubilee**, and it was quite an event. A royal jubilee is a celebration of the life and rule of a king or queen. These traditional grand celebrations are held every so often for a ruler in different countries and cultures all around the world.

The first recorded **Jubilees** were celebrated in the 1300s. These Christian celebrations began in the Catholic Church and focused on forgiveness and resolutions. Eventually, the tradition became associated with leadership and royalty. Royal jubilees evolved to celebrate the achievements, milestones, and lives of reigning monarchs.

FAST FACT

The last Royal Jubilee in the United Kingdom was in February of 2017. The ruling monarch, Queen Elizabeth II, celebrated her Sapphire Jubilee, or 65 years on the throne. Queen Elizabeth celebrated her Silver Jubilee in 1977, her Golden Jubilee in 2002, and her Diamond Jubilee in 2012.

Historically, very few English monarchs ruled or lived long enough to have jubilees. Victoria's reign changed that. A Silver Jubilee celebrates 25 years, a Golden Jubilee celebrates 50 years, and a Diamond Jubilee celebrates 60 years.

There are not many details about how the early kings of England partied at these celebrations, but Henry III, Edward III, James I, and James IV did reign long enough to celebrate 50-year jubilees. George III, Victoria's grandfather, celebrated his 50 years on the throne on October 25, 1809. The Golden Jubilee events included a private church service with his family, a thanksgiving dinner, and later, fireworks.

FAST FACT

In honor of the King George III's Golden Jubilee, the Earl of Buckinghamshire ordered a stone statue of the king to be built in Lincolnshire, England. The tall, lighthouse-like structure was called Dunston Pillar and could be seen for miles around. Unfortunately, during World War II, the pillar was taken down so that it wouldn't be struck by military aircraft. The top half of King George was salvaged and can be seen at Lincoln Castle today.

Victoria reigned long enough to have her first jubilee in 1862. It would have been a Silver Jubilee, but Albert had died at the end of 1861, just the year before, and the grieving widow was in no mood to celebrate anything without her companion by her side. When it came time for her 50th celebration, most of the people of the United Kingdom were excited and ready to honor her, and the festivities were awesome.

FAST FACT

The first king to have a public celebration for a 25-year Silver Jubilee was Victoria's grandson, George V, in 1935.

THE GOLDEN JUBILEE

Victoria celebrated her 50 years reigning as queen on June 20 and 21, 1887. She prepared for the grand ceremony the day before at Frogmore, the part of Windsor Castle where Albert was buried. In her diary, she wrote: "The day has come, and I am alone."[58] Seven of her surviving children would come, but two had already died.

After a quiet breakfast, Victoria took a train to Buckingham Palace to attend a royal banquet that would be held in her honor. That evening, the queen welcomed more than 50 guests and officials from all over the world, including leaders from the colonies and countries under the control of Great Britain. The kings of Denmark and Greece were there, as well as her sons and daughters. Everyone wore their finest and behaved their best. After the dinner, the company retired to the ballroom and listened to the queen's band play.

Later that night, Victoria wrote:

"Had a large family dinner. All the Royalties assembled in the Bow Room, and we dined in the Supper-room, which looked splendid with the buffet covered with the gold plate. The table was a large horseshoe one, with many lights on it."[59]

The jubilee celebrations ran two days, but celebrations around the country began earlier. There were sporting events, fairs, and picnics. Thousands of children were let out of school. Bonfires, dancing, and drinking spread all around the United Kingdom.

58. Baird, Julia. 2017.
59. Baird, Julia. 2017.

The next day, Tuesday, June 21st, was a more formal and exciting celebration. At Hyde Park, bands played, and theaters put on shows with actors and puppets. There were even animal shows with dogs, monkeys, and horses. The children and visitors snacked on meat pies and lemonade and played with balloons and thousands of other special Jubilee prizes, like jump ropes. Vendors sold souvenirs with the queen's face on every trinket and collectible imaginable.

FAST FACT: WELCOME TO THE PUNCH AND JUDY PUPPET SHOW!

Punch and Judy are a well-known hand-puppet show that came to England from Italy as early as the 1660s and were wildly popular during Victoria's reign. Originally, the puppets were marionettes, or puppets controlled with sticks and strings by an artist called the "punchman."

The act itself features short episodes of shocking comedy and violence, with Judy beating a poor victim on the head with her wooden club.

Most people found Punch and Judy funny, even though they were vicious. Even the popular Victorian writer, Charles Dickens, said,

"In my opinion the Street Punch is one of those extravagant reliefs from the realities of life which would lose its hold upon the people if it were made moral and instructive. I regard it as quite harmless in its influence and as an outrageous joke which no one in existence would think of regarding as an incentive to any kind of action or as a model for any kind of conduct."[60]

Punch and Judy were one of the more popular entertainments in Hyde Park during Queen Victoria's Golden Jubilee. During Victorian times, the more "modern" Punch and Judy shows featured music and sound effects, as well as a second man to round up an audience and collect money.

---

60. Dickens, Charles. 1849

That day, Queen Victoria donned her simple black mourning dress and a bonnet for the official celebration with her people. She refused to wear the traditional purple robes, and no royal crown rested on her head. Her only extravagance was a little white lace and a few sparkling diamonds added to her bonnet. She rode in an open **gilded** carriage through the city streets surrounded by a military entourage and some of the men in line to the throne in a victorious parade.

Queen Victoria looks off, stoic, at the
time of her Golden Jubilee.

FAST FACT

Three sons, nine grandsons, and five of Queen Victoria's sons-in-law escorted her carriage with the Indian Calvary.

The queen's **landau** was pulled by half a dozen ivory horses and escorted by an exotic Indian Calvary in bright ceremonial dress. One record states that 17 princes from Russia, Britain, Prussia, and other countries also attended. The American storyteller and writer of *Huckleberry Fin*, Mark Twain, was also there and remarked that the Indian princes stood out against the other leaders from British colonies and the Indian cavalry "attracted much attention."

People stretched for a far as the eye could see. At least 10 miles of benches were built for the parade route. A ceremony in Westminster Abbey would sit 10,000. Cheering well-wishers followed the queen for miles. Their heartfelt congratulations made her cry. She thanked them when she arrived at the palace by appearing on the balcony and waving to the crowds.

The day didn't end there. 43 members of Victoria's family were in attendance for the special event. She met with them and presented Jubilee brooches to her daughters and pins to her sons. A surviving pin that would have gone to her son Leopold, had he still been alive, is made of gold with 13 diamonds and seven rubies.

After private time with her children, Victoria prepared for another state banquet. She changed into a silver gown with roses and shamrocks and went to dinner. The meal ended with a receiving line where the queen personally met each guest, and then the party retired for a giant fireworks display outside the palace. The queen was wheeled out in her **pony chair** because she could no longer walk comfortably at 68-years-old.

An outdoor jubilee precession depicts a sign that reads, "Victoria Our Queen," as she was carried through the streets in her gilded carriage.

FAST FACT

A pony chair was like the bath chair invented around 1750 to push the ill or elderly around, especially at the seaside. Queen Victoria's pony chair was a comfortable, low seat with large wheels in the back and small wheels in the front with room for a small pony to pull it. A folding hood protected the queen from sun or bad weather, and a handbrake ensured she would be safe should the pony try to run off.

Everyone considered the Golden Jubilee a great success. It not only celebrated Victoria's long reign, but many other good things were accomplished in honor of the event. A Women's Jubilee Fund raised £75,000. Many people were released from prison at the queen's command. Of the few sentences that would not be excused, one was cruelty to animals. Victoria refused to show any leniency to those who tortured animals.

FAST FACT

On the night of Queen Victoria's Golden Jubilee, spectators saw London light up with all kinds of electric and gaslights, in addition to glowing candlesticks. To add to the magical night, not only were fireworks shot off, but a Mr. Breidenback of London also shot colored perfume 50 feet up into the air.[61] The fragrance smelled like violets.

Almost 70 years old and disabled, Queen Victoria's mind worked as sharp as ever. Life expectancy at this the time averaged around 45 years old. Few could have predicted that she would rule for another 14 years, but Little Drina did just that.

---

61. Baird, Julia. 2017.

THE HISTORY OF JUBILEE SOUVENIRS

One of the ways the people celebrated the jubilees of Queen Victoria was by collecting and trading souvenirs made especially for the occasion. The first collectibles for royal events were made for Charles II when he was restored to the throne in 1660. Coins, stamps, ceramic dishes, and pottery have endured as the most popular collectibles.

A coin *minted* in both sterling silver and copper-nickel was sold for collectors during Victoria's Silver Jubilee. Stamped into the metal was Queen Victoria on a horse. During her Golden Jubilee in 1887, commemorative coins were issued with her profile wearing a gown, pearls, and crown. At the time of the celebration, the coins were worth about five shillings, which was less than a U.S. dollar.

Jubilee stamps were released for the first time for Victoria's Golden Jubilee. Featuring her profile, they were the first stamps ever printed in two different colors. Wildly popular, the stamps were collected just like commemorative teapots, teacups, and other ceramics. Other products manufactured for her jubilees included handkerchiefs, tobacco pipes, clothing, and even wallpaper.

DIAMOND JUBILEE

In 1896, Great Britain celebrated 60 years of rule under Queen Victoria. She'd surpassed her grandfather as the longest ruling monarch the year before in September, setting another record for the once-teenage queen. The 60th-year mark fell under a Diamond Jubilee. Newspapers gloried her work and the coming event.

After so much time and success, Queen Victoria had become famous and admired around the world. Others used her as the benchmark for making comparisons; Americans compared Abraham Lincoln to her greatness and wisdom. Strangely, even some of the native people in colonies ruled by

Victoria worshiped her. Her image was stamped on keepsakes and in the minds of her subjects. Mark Twain wrote that no other in monarch in history had seen so much progress and invention.

The Diamond Jubilee began on June 20, 1897 with a private thanksgiving service for family only at Windsor Castle. Victoria did not want as big a celebration as her Golden Jubilee. She felt there was too much inconvenience for the city and the people, plus she had no intention of paying for it. The queen ordered the guest list to be pared down; no other kings or queens would be invited in order to keep it simple. The jubilee would focus instead on its colonies and people. It would be titled the **Festival of the British Empire**.

FAST FACT

Victoria's grandson, Wilhelm II, was not invited to the Jubilee, and he felt hurt and angry. As German Emperor and King of Prussia, he fought against his grandmother's country years after her death during World War I.

On June 22, just after 11 a.m., a cannon fired from within Hyde Park to announce the queen's royal carriage departure from Buckingham Palace. Observers noted that at the same time, the cloudy skies cleared and bright sunshine lit up the town. The city looked like a postcard with bright red and blue Union Jack flags and colorful flowers decorating buildings, windows, and lampposts. The queen proceeded through the streets of London to St. Paul's Cathedral for a public ceremony. Millions of admirers called or sang out *God Save the Queen!* and brought the widowed monarch to tears.

Once again, Queen Victoria poses stoically for a photo during her Diamond Jubilee.

FAST FACT

More champagne was imported in for the jubilee than an any other time in British history.[62]

Besides Albert, Victoria's late children Alice and Leopold were not there. The queen, with only seven surviving children, wore her traditional black as eight cream-colored horses pulled her carriage along the six-mile route. There were 17 carriages in all, carrying royal family members and leaders from Britain's colonies. Soldiers lined the sides of the road with their sharp bayonets pointed upright toward the sky to protect her.

An image of Queen Victoria's Diamond Jubilee on Parliament Hill.

62. Baird, Julia. 2017.

FAST FACT

Royal jubilees are traditionally held at St. Paul's Cathedral, a church of prayer dedicated to Saint Paul that was built between 1675 and 1710. It sits on the highest point of the city of London, thus Queen Victoria chose the location for the ceremony of her Diamond Jubilee there in 1897. George V celebrated his Silver Jubilee there in 1935, and Elizabeth II held her Silver, Golden, and Diamond jubilees there in 1977, 2002, and 2012, respectively.

At this time in her life, Victoria had to be carried from room to room by her favorite Indian servants. She'd never recovered from her fall before John Brown died, and now she suffered from arthritis and other painful conditions. To attend the jubilee without creating distractions or sympathy, Victoria decided to remain in her open-air carriage. The Archbishop of Canterbury and choir conducted the ceremony outside on the cathedral stairs; a program that only lasted for 20 minutes with the queen protected under a modest black parasol. After the ceremony, the crowded streets broke into cheers again for their longest-ruling queen.

FAST FACT

Even after she was elderly, Queen Victoria did not shy away from the modern technology of the age. She sent a telegraphed message to her subjects throughout the kingdom: "*From my heart I thank my beloved people. May God bless them. V.R. & I.*" A great many of her people had never known any other king or queen in their lifetime.

That day, Victoria returned to Buckingham through London and the adoring throngs. Even as the queen went to bed after the long day of celebrations, fireworks, bonfires, parties, and dancing continued into the early
hours of the next morning. A touched queen recorded in her journal: "*The
cheering was quite deafening, and every face seemed to be filled with real joy.*"[63]

63. Klein, Christopher. 2012

CHAPTER 10

The Queen's Final Days

Queen Victoria turned 80 years old in 1899. She worked hard and kept busy minding the affairs of the kingdom through military decisions and influence. It was a difficult year for the queen. Her third child and son, Alfie, died of throat cancer in February. Shortly thereafter, war broke out in Africa.

The **Anglo-Boer War** was an African war between the United Kingdom and two African states fighting to rid their countries of British imperialistic rule. The South African Republic and the Orange Free State used **guerilla warfare** to run the British out of their country. English residents, whether they were abroad for business, charity, or for the military, were affected by the violence.

The aging queen fought to have her say in the military decisions, but Parliament and her cabinet made moves without her. She made her displeasure known when the army's Commander-in-Chief was replaced without her input. She spent her free time knitting hats and scarves to be sent to her men, along with chocolates.

FAST FACT

England fought many wars in Africa to control territory. There were, in fact, two Anglo-Boer wars over British expansion, annexation, and opposition to British rule. The First Anglo-Boer occurred from 1880 to 1881 between British colonizers and the Boers from the Transvaal Republic. The Boers were joined by the Orange Free State. The second war began in 1899 between the same three countries and lasted until 1902. Often, the British were more confident than they were prepared to fight. Millions of Africans died in conquest for their lands.

The stress over her duties and the bloody, unpopular war began to wear on Victoria, and her health declined. Although she spent much of 1900 visiting the wounded in hospitals and studying telegraphs from her officials on the warfront, she could not sleep at night and lost interest in eating. Doctors and those close to Victoria became concerned as she grew thin and weak. Her vision became clouded by **cataracts**. There was little to cheer her or make her feel comfortable. Her duties became almost unbearable.

Those around Queen Victoria tried to keep the horrible news of war crimes and other atrocities committed by British soldiers out of her reach. Bad news depressed her. By the end of the year, Victoria was in pain, using strong opiates and sleeping a great deal of the time.

Dr. James Reid had already been given instructions for the care of Victoria's remains when it came time for her to pass. By the middle of January, he sent a note to her oldest son, Bertie. Bertie didn't always get along with Victoria, but he arrived at Osbourne House on January 19 to see a mother who wished for him only to "kiss her face."[64]

---

64. Baird, Julia. 2017

FAST FACT

It is not widely known that Dr. James Reid and Queen Victoria were close friends. Reid was the son of a Scottish vet who had a local education and only practiced in London a short time after studying advanced medicine in Germany. In 1881, Queen Victoria needed a doctor who spoke German as well as English, to help members of her extended family. Reid, having learned German, was hired and fit into the royal family so well the queen made him Physician-in-Ordinary by 1889. This title made him the official family doctor. The pair of them loved to discuss their love of animals and disgust of Prime Minister William Gladstone. The loyal Dr. Reid took many of Queen Victoria's secrets to the grave.

The queen grew weaker and slept most of the time. Her children began to arrive to say their goodbyes. Within two days, Bertie stood vigil over Victoria's bed with his sisters, Helena, Louise, and Beatrice. Victoria's beloved eldest daughter, Vicky, was fighting a painful battle with cancer in Prussia.

On January 22nd, the queen lay hardly breathing. A bishop and local priest stood at her bedside reciting prayers. She stubbornly clung to life until later in the afternoon. Around five o'clock she died in the arms of her grandson, Wilhelm, and her family doctor, Dr. Reid.

FAST FACT

Queen Victoria's daughter, Vicky, succumbed to cancer in Germany in August of 1901, less than 10 months after her mother's death. When Queen Victoria became ill in January of that year, Vicky's original breast cancer had spread to her spine. The eldest daughter of Victoria could only write letters, despairing that she was too sick and in too much pain to visit her mother to whom she was so close.

Outside Osbourne House, reporters caught wind of the news and set off down the road crying for all to hear that the queen had passed on to immortality. The next few weeks would bring quiet, sobbing crowds together wondering what would become of the United Kingdom and themselves.

 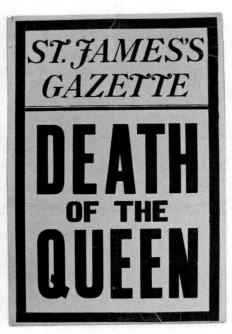

(Left) A proclamation for a day of mourning and (right) the cover of the St. James's Gazette alert her subjects to the death of Queen Victoria.

THE LONGEST RULING QUEEN

Queen Victoria planned her own funeral. Her trustworthy doctor and friend, Dr. Reid, carried out her private wishes and demands. Many of her secrets went with her to her final resting place and remained private for over 100 years.

After her white-covered coffin traveled by train back to London, Victoria was buried next to Albert at Frogmore on February 4, 1901, amid lightly falling snow. She had ordered a simple, elegant funeral. White horses would pull her carriage. Only her officers and bagpipe players from the Highlands would escort her coffin.

Inside her casket, Victoria's body had been clothed in a white dressing gown decorated only with the Order of the Garter; its royal blue sash draped across her chest from her left shoulder to the right side of her small waist. A veil covered her small face and was surrounded by white flowers. She looked, those who saw her last remembered, like a beautiful statue.

Unknown at the time, the queen took her family and the loves of her life with her into eternity. Rings from Albert, her mother and sister, and her daughters were buried with her. She also took the ring of John Brown, her old Highland friend, with her to the grave. Photographs of Albert, her children, and Brown, as well as shawls and handkerchiefs of those she loved were alongside her. A lock of Brown's hair was wrapped in her hand with gauze and camouflaged with flowers. The queen's final request for her people was that no black be worn or draped around the city in mourning. She wished for only gold and white to be draped in respectful memory. Until 2015, she would be remembered and revered as England's longest ruling monarch and queen.

Grandmother of Europe

While Queen Victoria was given several nicknames — Little Drina, Mrs. Melbourne, Widow of Windsor, and Mrs. Brown — the most renowned and respected nickname of the queen is *Grandmother of Europe*. This nickname was given to Victoria for more than one reason. She was a sweet, humble, grandmotherly figure to those around the world as she ruled with wisdom and humility.

Even in her final days, the wars of the past and horrific battles in Africa did not damage Victoria's angelic image in the eyes of her supporters. Despite the shift in the role of the monarchy in her lifetime, as well as government reforms pushed by republicans and socialists, she maintained her role as a ruler, stubbornly holding on to what she considered her right to change or influence.

She was also, through her nine children, literally the Grandmother of Europe. Most of Victoria's children married into royal families across Europe, Scandinavia, and Russia. Her grandchildren carried on the tradition, which made her grandson, Wilhelm II, the German Emperor.

In her lifetime and beyond, the granddaughters of Queen Victoria also ruled throughout Europe. Maud became Queen Consort of Norway, Alexandra became Czarina of Russia, and another granddaughter, Sophie, became Queen of Greece. Eugenie became Queen of Spain, and Marie married King Ferdinand of Romania.

The hemophilia gene

In 1853, Victoria gave birth to her son, Leopold, who would not be a healthy baby. She worried about him as a toddler when he did not grow or thrive. At eight years old, Leopold was diagnosed with a disease called **hemophilia**, but not much was known about it at the time.

This painting was commissioned a year before Queen Victoria's death.

Hemophilia is a condition where the blood will not clot, so bleeding continues whether it's happening inside or outside the body. At that time, it was believed that hemophiliacs suffered from weak veins. They did not live long, usually dying before they turned 20 years old.

Victoria worried herself sick over Leopold throughout his life. She was strict and controlling, leaving him little to do but read books so he became an academic scholar. By the time he lived to a miserable, quiet 25 years old, Leopold defied Victoria and got married, which was discouraged because it might pass on the sickness.

Like hemophilia, not much was known about genetics in the early years of Victoria's rule. She did not know when Leopold was diagnosed that females carried the DNA gene that passed on hemophilia and the type Leopold had only affected males.

Unfortunately, Leopold died in 1884 when he was 30 years old. The young father fell and injured his knee while on a trip to France. A few hours later he suffered a brain hemorrhage, or bleeding in the brain, and passed away, leaving behind a pregnant wife and one daughter.

FAST FACT

Queen Victoria's daughters, Princess Alice and Princess Beatrice — possibly even Princess Helena — passed on the hemophilia gene to the royal bloodlines of Russia and Spain.

As Grandmother of Europe, Victoria spread the hemophilia gene on to Europe and Russia through three of her daughters. Three grandchildren suffered from the disease, as well as a great-grandson who was heir to the Russian throne.

A modern great-great-granddaughter

On September 9, 2015, Queen Elizabeth II surpassed her great-great-grandmother, Queen Victoria, becoming the longest ruling monarch of the United Kingdom in history. Like her great-great-grandmother, Elizabeth II is known for her selfless life of public service.

FAST FACT

Queen Elizabeth II celebrated her Silver Jubilee in 1977, her Golden Jubilee in 2002, and her Diamond Jubilee in 2012. On February 6, 2017, the queen celebrated 65 years as ruling monarch with a Sapphire Jubilee. She commemorated the event with photographs taken of her wearing beautiful, blue sapphire jewels that were given to her by her father on her wedding day.

Elizabeth II was born on April 21, 1926, to the Duke and Duchess of York. She was third in line to the throne, and like Victoria, expected to live a rather normal life, not knowing what the future might hold. Unexpectedly, in 1936, her uncle, King Edward VII gave up the throne to marry a commoner, and Elizabeth's father, George VI, became king. Everything changed for Elizabeth as she became the next royal in line for the crown should her father pass away.

Queen Elizabeth II was christened Elizabeth Alexandra Mary on May 29, 1926. She grew up at with a younger sister, Margaret. The family had loving relationships and was very close. The young princess was educated at home. Like her great-great-grandmother, she studied history, law, French, art, and music. She was athletic, too, mastering such sports as swimming and horseback riding.

This formal portrait of Queen Elizabeth II was taken in 1959. She is wearing the Vladimir Tiara, the Queen Victoria Jubilee Necklace, the blue Garter Riband, Badge, and Garter Star, and the Royal Family Orders of King George V and King George VI.

FAST FACT

Elizabeth II has connections with over 600 different charities, focusing her work on youth, wildlife, and environmental issues.

In 1934, Elizabeth met Prince Phillip of Greece and Denmark at a relative's wedding, and they hit it off, becoming close friends and then sweethearts. They got engaged in 1947 and married in November of that year at Westminster Abbey.

FAST FACT

As the ruling monarch of the constitutional monarchy of the United Kingdom, Queen Elizabeth's duties include charity work and fundraisers; hosting heads of State at parties and receptions; and leading national celebrations and remembrances in honor of others who have contributed to good of England and its people.

Elizabeth and Phillip, who became Duke of Edinburg and is consort to the queen, had a family of four children: Prince Charles, Princess Anne, Prince Andrew, and Prince Edward. Elizabeth is known by her friends and family, especially her grandchildren and great-grandchildren, for her humor, kindness, and calm presence. Surely her great-great-grandmother, Victoria, would be proud.

CONCLUSION

Victoria's Final Word

The rule of Queen Victoria not only changed history in the United Kingdom, it affected people and governments around the entire world. By the time of her death, one-fourth of England's people lived in Canada, New Zealand, Australia, or Africa. England became a major force in modernization and progress and defended its people with an almost unstoppable army and navy.

FAST FACT

"The sun never sets on the British Empire" is a phrase used to describe the United Kingdom during Queen Victoria's reign that expanded England's territories. It meant that no matter what time of day it was, somewhere in the world, the sun was shining down on a British colony or territory. The phrase, "the sun never sets on..." originally described the Spanish Empire in the 16th century and thereafter until England began to come to world power about 300 years later.

In 1821, the Scottish newspaper, the Caledonian Mercury, boasted that, "On her dominions the sun never sets; before his evening rays leave the spires of Quebec, his morning beams have shone three hours on Port Jackson, and while sinking from the waters of Lake Superior, his eye opens upon the Mouth of the Ganges."

Time and England's queen had transformed the kingdom into a true constitutional monarchy where the people had representation, even abroad. The colonies of the United Kingdom were now self-governed with prime ministers.

This did not diminish the influence of a king or queen. A leader of the House of Commons, Arthur Balfour, claimed that the monarchy linked everyone together constitutionally and that Victoria was a "living symbol of imperial unity." He loudly supported the 1909 Royal Titles Act that added "and the dominions beyond the seas" to the monarchy's title, King of the United Kingdom of Great Britain and Ireland. Even in death, Victoria brought peoples of different backgrounds, races, religions, and addresses together under the symbolic station of King or Queen of England.

FAST FACT

At home and abroad, Victoria had become a Christian mother figure, and in some cultures, godlike. People of the Muslim and Hindu faiths prayed for her. Others revered her as a saint.

It was ironic that Victoria paid little attention to those who felt women should be allowed to vote, choose their careers, and own their own properties, for her legacy became a beacon for women's rights. She was a role model for those who wanted to both raise families and hold jobs. Her independence on the throne of England made women believe it was as natural for a woman to rule as it was a man.

Victoria had once said firmly that there should be "no such thing as women's work." She knew how to soften a man's heart so that he would listen, and she understood what it took to get what she wanted when it came to politics. In short, Victoria knew how to network and influence to get the results that she felt were right.

American women admired and envied her power and achievements. In America, women's rights advocates cried there were no longer any arguments that women could not successfully perform in politics or public duties.

FAST FACT

Critics of Queen Victoria's argue that she did not support women's rights in her own country, but only for herself. Although she was quick to defend women in her circle of friends and family, some of the greatest brutalities of war committed against women happened in the last year of her life in the South African wars. Never did she, critics point out, express concern for women who were widowed, assaulted, or murdered, during British battles for land and colonization around the world as the empire expanded.

Victoria was a profound and humble opposite of the English monarchs that came before her. She was sincerely religious, moral, honest, faithful, and true to her role as a wife and mother. Her focus on her royal duties meant a lifetime of rigorous work on paper, in meetings, and traveling abroad, all with public scrutiny and sometimes, criticism. Stopping only to meet her family's needs, Queen Victoria worked up until her final illness when she became unable to do so.

The queen was loved, admired, and remembered for her humble approach to life. It set an example for the rulers to come after her. She wore little when it came to accessories and dressed comfortably in her simple black dresses and bonnets. She expressed an awareness of her weaknesses to her husband and children, noting at her death, that she was not perfect but struggled with temper, pride, a control streak, and self-pity.

Despite her self-acknowledged weaknesses, Victoria never completely gave up when life was almost too much to bear. She endured life and reigned for decades, blossoming from a stubborn teen queen into the ruler of an empire.

Today, Queen Victoria is remembered as a woman who shouldered the burden of power with humility and dignity. She is a motherly — and grandmotherly — figure of graciousness, strength, and devotion. In her last days on earth, the people of England began to think of themselves as Victorians, and the term, "Victorian" came to describe the era. It was the closing chapter of one of the greatest empires on earth and a new dawn for rights and representation for all in the Old World.

Many books and films about Victoria have been written and produced to honor, and sometimes, examine, her memory. She is as popular a figurehead of Great Britain's history as she was while she was alive. The young queen, who went on to represent the people of the United Kingdom in widow's black, set the pattern for the ceremonial and constitutional responsibilities carried out by the crown today.

Despite the praise and criticism of this pioneering woman of the 19th century, willful and strong Victoria made certain that in death it would be she that would have the final word — to Albert and to her people. At her tomb, just above the door, a visitor can find the engraved words:

"Farewell best beloved, here at last I shall rest with thee,
with thee in Christ I shall rise again."

Author's Note

Whether it's pirate ships at sea or a twist of fate that thrusts an ordinary person like you or me into greatness, history is the foundation of the successes and failures that the world stands on today. We have so much to learn from it to make the world a better place.

There are not many traits more admirable than courage, honesty, loyalty, and humility. An impressively strong and powerful woman, Queen Victoria attempted to master them all and that made her as beloved to the world as she was criticized for her failings. When all is said and done, it is clear that she was only human just like the rest of us.

Through researching historical books that quote passages from her many journals, as well as studying the hundreds of pictures she made sure would immortalize her family, I've come to admire Victoria in more ways than I ever imagined. Her life was no fairytale. It wasn't fair and there weren't always happy endings, but she knew true love, and she sacrificed having a normal life in order serve the people of England and its colonies according to her conscience.

Queen Victoria's story is one of destiny, struggle, courage, and triumph. Intentional or not, she paved the way for humanity to embrace more kindness, more empathy, and more fairness. Her life as recorded in her diaries and in public record shows us not only that great things can happen to anyone, but that anyone can rise up to do what's right and to endure with honor.

The Life and Times of Queen Victoria

1818: Prince Edward, Duke of Kent, marries Victoire of Saxe-Coburg-Saalfield

1819: The future Queen Victoria is born and christened Princess Alexandrina Victoria, daughter of Edward, Duke of Kent, and Victoire of Saxe-Coburg-Saalfield

1820: Princess Victoria's father, the Duke of Kent, dies of a winter illness

1836: Princess Victoria meets Prince Albert of Saxe-Coburg

1837: Victoria becomes Queen of England at 18 years old after the death of her uncle, King William IV

1838: Victoria is crowned Queen of England at Westminster Abbey during her royal coronation

1839: Prince Albert visits Queen Victoria, and they fall in love

1840: Prince Albert marries Queen Victoria at St. James Palace

1840: Birth of Princess Victoria, Queen Victoria's oldest child

1840: The first assassination attempt on Queen Victoria

1841: Birth of Prince Albert Edward, the future King of England

1842:   Two attempted assassinations are made on the life of Queen Victoria.

1843:   Birth of Princess Alice Maude Mary

1844:   Birth of Prince Alfred Ernest Albert

1845:   Queen Victoria and Prince Albert buy Osbourne House on the Isle of Wight

1846:   Birth of Princess Helena Augusta Victoria

1848:   Birth of Princess Louise Caroline Alberta

1849:   Assassination attempt on Queen Victoria

1850:   Birth of Prince Arthur William Patrick

1851:   The Great Exhibition at the Crystal Palace

1852:   Prince Albert buys Balmoral Castle in Scotland

1853:   Birth of Prince Leopold George Duncan

1857:   Birth of Princess Beatrice Mary Victoria

1857:   Prince Albert is awarded the title of "Prince Consort"

1861:   Prince Albert dies of a long illness at 42-years-old

1872:   Assassination attempt on Queen Victoria

1877:   Victoria is titled the "Empress of India"

1882:   Assassination attempt on Queen Victoria

1883:   John Brown dies of a sudden illness

1887:   Queen Victoria celebrates her Golden Jubilee

1887:   Hafiz Mohammad Abdul Karim arrives in England and becomes the queen's "Munshi"

1897:   Queen Victoria celebrates her Diamond Jubilee

1901:   Queen Victoria passes away at Osborne House in her grandson's arms, on the Isle of Wight on January 22nd and is buried on a cold, snowy day.

People of Note

Alexander Graham Bell: a Scottish scientist, inventor, and engineer who patented the first telephone

Baroness Louise Lehzen: governess, teacher, advisor, companion, and closest friend of Queen Victoria during her childhood and up until she married Prince Albert

Caroline of Brunswick: the wife and Queen of King George IV, who died one year after her royal wedding; an aunt of Queen Victoria

Charles, Prince of Leiningen: the older half-brother of Queen Victoria who was born in 1804 and later became prime minister of the German empire

Florence Nightingale: the English founder of modern nursing born in 1820

George I: King of Great Britain and Ireland from 1714 to 1727

George II: King of Great Britain and Ireland between 1727 and 1760; the great-grandfather of Queen Victoria.

George III: The grandfather of Queen Victoria; King of Great Britain and King of Ireland from 1760 until 1820 and the third British monarch from

Germany's House of Hanover, although he was born in England and never visited Hanover

Hafiz Mohammad Abdul Karim: the infamous Indian attendant, servant, and secretary who served Queen Victoria the last 15 years of her life

Lady Florence Dixie: a Scottish explorer, war correspondent, writer, and feminist

Lord Dalhousie: the title of Englishman, James Andrew Broun-Ramsay, also known as Lord Ramsay, who served as a Scottish statesman, colonial administrator in British India, and later, as Governor-General of India from 1848 to 1856

Napoleon Bonaparte: a French statesman and military leader who rose to power during the French Revolution and later crowned himself Emperor of France; led the Napoleonic Wars until he was defeated and ultimately exiled

Prince Albert of Saxe-Coburg: the beloved husband of Queen Victoria who ruled by her side as Prince Consort

Prince Carl: another name for Charles, Prince of Leiningen, who was Queen Victoria's older half-brother

Prince Leopold of Saxe-Coburg-Saalfeld: the beloved advisor and uncle of Queen Victoria who was born a German prince in 1790 in Coburg and later became first King of Belgium; married Princess Charlotte of Wales, the only legitimate child of the King George IV and second in line to the British throne

Princess Alexandrina Victoria: the full name of Queen Victoria

Princess Feodora: Queen Victoria's half-older sister who was born Anna Feodora Auguste Charlotte Wilhelmine in 1807

Princess Victoire of Saxe-Coburg-Saalfeld: a German princess born in 1786 who became the mother of Queen Victoria; died in 1861 and buried at the church of Windsor Castle

Queen Charlotte: The wife of King George III and grandmother of Queen Victoria. Known as Charlotte of Mecklenburg-Strelitz, she was born in 1708 in a German area of the Holy Roman Empire; died in 1752

William the Conqueror: the first Norman King of England who ruled from 1066 to 1087

Glossary

1st Battalion of Scots Fusiliers: an infantry regiment of the British Army that existed from 1678 until 1959

2nd Regiment of Life Guards: a cavalry (a military unit on horseback) regiment in the British Army formed in 1788 by joining together the 2nd Troop of Horse Guards and the 2nd Troop of Horse Grenadier Guards

Admiral of the Fleet: the highest rank in the British Royal Navy

Albert Memorial: an ornate canopy standing 175 feet high in Kensington Gardens, London, with a statue of Prince Albert. It cost £120,000 and took 10 years to build

Anglo-Boer War: a war fought between the United Kingdom and two African Boer states

Anglo-Saxons: Germanic tribes who inhabited Great Britain beginning around the 5th century

autocrat: a king or queen who claims absolute power

Balmoral Castle: a large stone mansion house with towers and turrets located in Aberdeenshire, Scotland

bobbies: police officers in England

Buckingham Palace: the official London residence of the reigning King or Queen of England

cartridge: a bullet

cast: a mold of a shape or form

cataracts: a clouding of the lens of the eye

chamberlain: an assisting officer who manages the household of the king

Claremont House: a two-story Greek and Romance style 18th-century mansion in Surrey, England; the former residence of Princess Charlotte and Queen Victoria's Uncle Leopold, and later Victoria's son, Prince Leopold

commoner: an ordinary person with no rank or royal title

constitutional monarchy: a form of government with a constitutionally organized lower government, and a king or queen where the ruler does not have absolute power but follows rules, laws, and traditions that are established, written or unwritten

coronation: the official ceremony that crowns a king or queen

Danube: a region and famous river in Germany

Diamond Jubilee: a 60th anniversary celebration

Doctrine of Lapse: a policy of the East India Trading Company up to 1858 that seized the Indian property of anyone who died without an heir

Duke of Kent: a title created for royals of the United Kingdom who carry out military and civil duties

Duke of York: a royal title for nobles and aristocrats usually given to the second son of a king or queen

East India Trading Company: an English trading company formed in 1600 to pursue and conduct trade with the Chinese and India

Enfield musket: a .577 caliber muzzle-loading rifled musket used by the British Empire from 1853 to 1867 and thought to be more accurate

erysipelas: a serious infection that comes with a skin rash

exile: banishment; to be barred from entering or living in one's own native land

Festival of the British Empire: another name used today for a British jubilee

forensics: scientific tests used to solve crimes

gaols: jail or prison

ghillie: a Scottish man or boy who accompanies someone on a hunting trip

gilded: gold; gold-plated, or covered in gold

Golden Jubilee: a 50th anniversary celebration.

governess: traditionally, a woman hired to educate and train children in a family home

Great Exhibition of 1851, or The Great Exhibition of the Works of Industry of All Nations: the first World Fair that encouraged exhibitions from around the world

guerilla warfare: the use of a small, mobile force that depends on the support of locals and takes advantage of local terrain and geography

hemophilia: an inherited health problem that affects the blood's ability to clot or stop

Hindustani: a dialect from northwest India; usually called Hindi or Urdu

House of Hanover: a German royal dynasty, or family line, whose heirs ruled the German Kingdom of Hanover, as well as Great Britain and Ireland, from 1714 until Queen Victoria's death in 1901

indigenous: original; native

Industrial Revolution: a period of new manufacturing processes that led to new inventions and technology from as early as 1760 to about 1840

jubilee: an anniversary celebration

mausoleum: a tomb

Ladies of the Bedchamber: the official title of a royal lady-in-waiting who assists the queen

Lake Albert: one of the African Great Lakes in Uganda and the Democratic Republic of the Congo

landau: a type of four-wheeled carriage with two roof sections that can be detached. The front and back passenger seats face each other

Married Women's Property Act 1882: an act of Parliament that allowed married women to own and control their own property

monarch: a head of state, usually a king or queen, in a sovereign nation

Monroe Doctrine: an 1823 American policy that opposed any new British colonization in North America

mudlarks: a person who scavenges lake or riverbanks to find anything valuable to use or sell

Mughul emperors: rulers of the Indian subcontinent between the 16th and 18th centuries

Napoleonic Wars: A series of wars for territory and land between France and the United Kingdom and allies that lasted from 1803 until 1815 and cost millions of lives

newsvendor: a person who sells newspapers

Normans: people of Normandy, France, who descended from Vikings and came to power in England around the 10th century

opium: a highly addictive drug used since 3400 B.C; useful for managing pain, it's acquired from the opium poppy seed pod

Order of the Garter: an order of chivalry, or bravery, founded by Edward III in the year 1348 and considered the most prestigious British order of chivalry in England and the United Kingdom

Osbourne House: a large estate with towers standing in East Cowes on the Isle of Wight; rebuilt between 1845 and 1851 for Queen Victoria and Prince Albert

Parliament: the supreme legislative body of the United Kingdom

Peel's Brimstone: a nickname for corn maize shipped from India to the United Kingdom to aid the population during the Irish potato famine

peninsula: a piece of land almost completely surrounded by water on at least three sides

pension: an allowance of money usually for retirement

poaching: hunting animals out of season or on private property

poorhouse: a government-run house that required work for food and shelter

pony chair: a small, light carriage for one person with a folding hood that is pushed by a person or pulled by a pony

Prime Minister: the head of the government in the United Kingdom that presides over Parliament

Prince Regent: a prince who rules a monarchy but without the title of king

Privy Council: an official group of aristocratic advisers to the sovereign of the United Kingdom

Regency: the British era between the 18th and 19th centuries defined by elaborate art and living with Egyptian and Greek influences

representation: speaking, acting, and decision-making for a person or group of people

Royal Albert Hall: a concert hall in London that seats over 5,000 and holds annual summer concerts

Sevastopol: the largest city on today's Crimean peninsula and a major seaport on the Black Sea controlled by Russia

Silver Jubilee: a 25th anniversary celebration

social anxiety: a fear of social interaction or being around other people

sovereign: a monarch or ruler with great power

suffrage: the right to vote in an election

The Bedchamber Crisis: an early crisis in Queen Victoria's reign where she refused to work with her new prime minister, Robert Peel, by refusing to replace her Ladies of the Bedchamber who shared her own party politics

The House of Commons: the lower half of England's governing Parliament that meets at Westminster with representatives who have been elected

The House of Lords: the upper house of England's governing Parliament that meets at Westminster with aristocratic representatives who have inherited their positions

The Settlement Act of 1701: an act of Parliament passed in 1701 to give succession to the English and Irish crowns to Protestants only

tsar: a Russian title for emperor or king

Vikings: seafaring warriors from the late eighth to early 11th century that traded, fought, and attempted to take over Great Britain

War of 1812: a secondary war between the United States and Great Britain over territory and trade on the North American continent

Westminster Abbey: a Gothic-style abbey built in London in the 1500s, and the traditional London church used for royal ceremonies

Whig: a British reform party that desires a parliament with supreme power over the head of state, but supports a constitutional monarchy

Bibliography

"A History of Jubilees." https://www.royal.uk/history-jubilees. Web. December 2017.

Baird, Julia. *Victoria the Queen.* New York: Random House, 2017. Print.

Banerjee, A. "The Prince Consort and his Legacy: A Review of Albert: A Life, by Jules Stewart." The Victorian Web. www.victorianweb.org. April 2012. Web. October 2017.

Barnes, Alison. "The First Christmas Tree." History Today, Volume 56, Issue 12. December 2006. http://www.historytoday.com/alison-barnes/first-christmas-tree. Web. December 2017.

Barrett, Charlotte. "Victoria Publishing History." University of Oxford. https://writersinspire.org/content/victorian-publishing-history. Web. December 2017.

Bigham, Clive. *The Prime Ministers of Britain.* 1923.

Bogdanor, Vernon. "Queen Victoria." Transcript. https://www.gresham.ac.uk/lectures-and-events/queen-victoria#D4ecZ0yxH7WoRsqd.99. 20 September 2016. Web. December 2017.

Broad, Georgie. "How the Other Half Lived: Rich and Poor Women in Victorian Britain." History is Now Magazine. http://www.historyis

nowmagazine.com/blog/2014/4/21/how-the-other-half-lived-rich-and-poor-women-in-victorian-britain#.WkQohjdOnZs. 21April 2014. Web. December 2017.

"Cavalier King Charles Spaniel." American Kennel Club. http://www.akc. org/dog-breeds/cavalier-king-charles-spaniel/. Web. October 2017.

Cohen, Jennie. "A Brief History of Bloodletting." History.com. http:// www.history.com/news/a-brief-history-of-bloodletting. May 30, 2012. Web. October 2017.

"Death and funeral of Prince." *The New Zealand Spectator and Cook's Strait Guardian*, Saturday, March 22, 1862. Victoria University of Wellington. http://nzetc.victoria.ac.nz/tm/scholarly/tei-NZSpec18620322-t1-body-d1.html. 2016. Web. December 2017.

"Death of Prince Albert." History in an Hour. http://www.historyinan-hour.com/2011/12/14/death-of-prince-albert/. 14 December 2011. Web. November 2017.

Dugdale-Pointon, T. (16 November 2000), Napoleonic Wars (1799-1815), http://www.historyofwar.org/articles/wars_napoleonic.html. Web. November 2017.

Eschner, Kat. "The Eight Assassination Attempts on Queen Victoria Just Made Her More Powerful." Smithsonian Magazine. https://www. smithsonianmag.com/smart-news/eight-assassination-attempts-queen-victoria-just-made-her-more-powerful. 30 May 2017. Web. December 2017.

"First War of Indian Independence." New World Encyclopedia, 11 Apr 2017, 23:21 UTC. http://www.newworldencyclopedia.org/p/index. php?title=First_War_of_Indian_Independence&oldid=1004272. Web. December 2017.

"Florence Nightingale." Biography.com. https://www.biography.com/people/florence-nightingale-9423539. 28 April 2017. Web. December 2017.

Foot, Michael Richard Daniell. "William Ewart Gladstone." Encyclopædia Britannica, Inc. https://www.britannica.com/biography/William-Ewart-Gladstone. Web. November 2017.

Gallop, Adrian. "Mortality improvements and evolution of life expectancies." www.osfi-bsif.gc.ca/eng/docs/deip_gallop.pdf. Web. December 2017.

"George III." Biography.com. The Biography.com. https://www.biography.com/people/king-george-iii. 20 July 2015. Web. November 2017.

Gigliotti, Jim. *Who was Queen Victoria?* Turtleback Books: 2014. Print.

Hibbert, Christopher. "Queen Victoria and her Prime Ministers." BBC. http://www.bbc.co.uk/history/british/victorians/victoria_ministers_01.shtml. 17 February 2011. Web. November 2017.

Johnson, Ben. "Kings and Queens of England & Britain." www.historic-uk.com. http://www.historic-uk.com/HistoryUK/KingsQueensofBritain/. Web. October 2017.

Klein, Christopher. "8 Times Queen Victoria Survived Attempted Assassinations." History.com. http://www.history.com/news/history-lists/eight-times-queen-victoria-survived-attempted-assassinations. 30 May 2017. Web. December 2017.

Klein, Christopher. "Queen Victoria's Diamond Jubilee." History.com. http://www.history.com/news/queen-victorias-diamond-jubilee. 2012. Web. December 2017.

Major, Joanne. "The Dunston Pillar: celebrating the 50 year reign of King George III." All Things Georgian. https://georgianera.wordpress.com/

tag/george-iii-golden-jubilee-1809/. 23 October 2014. Web. December 2017.

Martin, Sir Theodore. *Queen Victoria As I Knew Her*. Edinburg and London: William Blackwood and Sons, 958.

Moniek. "In her Sister's Shadow, Feodora of Leiningen." History of Royal Women. https://www.historyofroyalwomen.com/the-royal-women/queen-victorias-siblings/ 28 September 2015. Web. October 2017.

Parkinson, Caroline. "Men's average height 'up 11cm since 1870s'." BBC News. http://www.bbc.com/news/health-23896855. 2 September 2013. Web. November 2017.

Picard, Liza. "Education in Victorian Britain." Victorian Britain. https://www.bl.uk/victorian-britain/articles/the-great-exhibition. 14 October, 2009. Web. November 2017.

Picard, Liza. "The Great Exhibition." Victorian Britain. https://www.bl.uk/victorian-britain/articles/the-great-exhibition. 14 October, 2009. Web. November 2017.

Price, Paxton. "Victorian Child Labor and the Conditions They Worked In." Victorian Children. https://victorianchildren.org/victorian-child-labor/. 2 March 2013. Web. December 2017.

Sitwell, Edith. *Victoria of England*. London: Bloomsbury Publishing Pl, 1936. Print.

SparkNotes Editors. "SparkNote on Queen Victoria." SparkNotes.com. SparkNotes LLC. 2005. Web. 3 Jan. 2018.

The British Newspaper Archive. "Alexander Graham Bell demonstrates the telephone to Queen Victoria." In Headlines from History. https://blog.britishnewspaperarchive.co.uk/2013/03/03/alexander-graham-bell/. March 3, 2013. Web. December 2017.

The Editors of Encyclopædia Britannica. "Industrial Revolution." Encyclopædia Britannica, Inc. 2 May 2017. https://www.britannica.com/event/Industrial-Revolution. Web. October 2017.

The Editors of Encyclopædia Britannica. "Napoleonic Wars." Encyclopædia Britannica. 22 February 2017. https://www.britannica.com/event/Napoleonic-Wars. Web. November 2017.

"The empire on which the sun never sets." World Heritage Encyclopedia. World Heritage. http://self.gutenberg.org/articles/eng/The_empire_on_which_the_sun_never_sets. Web. December 2017.

Trueman, C.N. "The Victoria Cross" historylearningsite.co.uk. The History Learning Site, 6 Mar 2015. Web. December 2017.

"Queen Victoria and the Bonapartes." http://www.thistlepublishing.co.uk. Web. November 2017.

"Queen Victoria's Children." English Heritage. http://www.english-heritage.org.uk/visit/places/osborne/things-to-see-and-do/queen-victorias-children/. Web. November 2017.

"Sentences and Punishments." Victorian Crime and Punishment. http://vcp.e2bn.org/justice/section2194-sentences-and-punishments.html. Web. December 2017.

"Victorian Occupations: Life and Labor in the Victorian Period as Seen by Artists, Writers, and Modern Historians." The Victorian Web. www.victorianweb.org. 5 March 2017. Web. December 2017.

Wilkinson, Philip. *The British Monarchy for Dummies.* 2006. Print.

Williams, Kate. *Becoming Queen Victoria.* Ballantine Books: 2010. Print.

Young, R. "Portrait of Queen Victoria and Princess Beatrice of the United Kingdom." Napoleon.org. July 2017. Web. November 2017.

Index

Author's Bio

D anielle Thorne is the author of a dozen historical and contemporary books and adventures. From pirates to presidents, and queens, too, she loves to blog, research, and travel the U.S. and Caribbean. Some of her work has appeared in places like *Mississippi Crow*, *The Nantahala Review*, and *StorySouth*. She has edited, co-chaired writing competitions, and judged contests for young adults and published authors.

Mrs. Thorne loves meeting readers and writers of all ages from around the world through conferences and social media. She is a BYU-Idaho graduate, youth leader, certified diver, half-hearted runner, and unofficial foodie. Currently, she is working on a young adult pirate adventure while enjoying life south of Atlanta, Georgia, with a Mr. Thorne and fuzzy cat. Visit her at **www.daniellethorne.com**.